The
Shawnee

The
Shawnee

Titles in the Indigenous Peoples of North America series include:

The
Shawnee

Mary C. Wilds

LUCENT
BOOKS ®

THOMSON

GALE

San Diego • Detroit • New York • San Francisco • Cleveland • New Haven, Conn. • Waterville, Maine • London • Munich

THOMSON

GALE

LIBRARY OF CONGRESS CATALOGING-IN-PUBLICATION DATA

Wilds, Mary C. 1960–
    The Shawnee / by Mary C. Wilds.
    p. cm. — (Indigenous peoples of North America)
    Summary: Discusses the origins, ceremonies, festivals, and leadership of the Shawnee
    people, as well as their relationships with European settlers.
    Includes bibliographical references and index.
        ISBN 1-59018-090-9 (alk. paper)
        1. Shawnee Indians—History—Juvenile literature. 2. Shawnee Indians—Social life
    and customs—Juvenile literature. [1. Shawnee Indians. 2. Indians of North America—
    East (U.S.)] I. Title. II. Series.
    E99.S35W55 2003
    974.004'973—dc21
                                                                    2003000411

Printed in the United States of America

Contents

Foreword

North America's native peoples are often relegated to history—viewed primarily as remnants of another era—or cast in the stereotypical images long found in popular entertainment and even literature. Efforts to characterize Native Americans typically result in idealized portrayals of spiritualists communing with nature or bigoted descriptions of savages incapable of living in civilized society. Lost in these unfortunate images is the rich variety of customs, beliefs, and values that comprised—and still comprise—many of North America's native populations.

The Indigenous Peoples of North America series strives to present a complex, realistic picture of the many and varied Native American cultures. Each book in the series offers historical perspectives as well as a view of contemporary life of individual tribes and tribes that share a common region. The series examines traditional family life, spirituality, interaction with other native and non-native peoples, warfare, and the ways the environment shaped the lives and cultures of North America's indigenous populations. Each book ends with a discussion of life today for the Native Americans of a given region or tribe.

In any discussion of the Native American experience, there are bound to be similarities. All tribes share a past filled with unceasing white expansion and resistance that led to more than four hundred years of conflict. One U.S. administration after another pursued this goal and fought Indians who attempted to defend their homelands and ways of life. Although no war was ever formally declared, the U.S. policy of conquest precluded any chance of white and Native American peoples living together peacefully. Between 1780 and 1890, Americans killed hundreds of thousands of Indians and wiped out whole tribes.

The Indians lost the fight for their land and ways of life, though not for lack of bravery, skill, or a sense of purpose. They simply could not contend with the overwhelming numbers of whites arriving from Europe or the superior weapons they brought with them. Lack of unity also contributed to the defeat of the Native Americans. For most, tribal identity was more important than racial identity. This loyalty left the Indians at a distinct disadvantage. Whites had a strong racial identity and they fought alongside each other even when there was disagreement, because they shared a racial destiny.

Although all Native Americans share this tragic history they have many distinct differences. For example, some tribes and individuals sought to cooperate almost immediately with the U.S. government while others steadfastly resisted the white presence. Life before the arrival of white settlers also varied. The nomads of the Plains developed altogether different lifestyles and customs from the fishermen of the Northwest coast.

Contemporary life is no different in this regard. Many Native Americans—forced onto reservations by the American government—struggle with poverty, poor health, and inferior schooling. But others have regained a sense of pride in themselves and their heritage, enabling them to search out new routes to self-sufficiency and prosperity.

The Indigenous Peoples of North America series attempts to capture the differences as well as similarities that make up the experiences of North America's native populations—both past and present. Fully documented primary and secondary source quotations enliven the text. Sidebars highlight events, personalities, and traditions. Bibliographies provide readers with ideas for further research. In all, each book in this dynamic series provides students with a wealth of information as well as launching points for further research.

A Southern People

The Shawnee Indians were known as wanderers. Over a period of many years small groups of Shawnee moved from territory to territory, across Midwestern prairies and the mountains of the southeast, as far west as Illinois, as far east as South Carolina, and as far south as Alabama. But these tribal migrations were not always voluntary: The Shawnee were frequently caught up in bloody conflicts not of their own doing. One of the earliest was the Beaver Wars.

During the 1600s, the Iroquois Confederacy of central New York declared war on the Huron Indians and other tribes in the Great Lakes region. The fierce fighting forced the Shawnee from their home territory of southern Ohio, northern Kentucky, western Pennsylvania, and West Virginia. More than forty years after the Beaver Wars, however, the Shawnee began migrating back to the Ohio River valley—the region to which the Shawnee owe their roots.

Ancient Settlements

Historians believe that the earliest Shawnee were part of a prehistoric tribe known as the Fort Ancient culture. Fort Ancients first appeared in southern Ohio, southern Indiana, northern Kentucky, and western Virginia circa A.D. 1000. Like the Shawnee, they built circular or rectangular houses covered in bark. They hunted, fished, gathered plants and berries, planned their communities near rivers, and grew corn, beans, and squash.

The Fort Ancient culture died out around 1650, a time when the Shawnee were flourishing in the region. The fate of the Ancients, as well as the rise of the Shawnee, is shrouded in mystery since neither group had a written language. By the time French explorer Jacques Marquette encountered the Shawnee during an Ohio River expedition in 1673, they were a thriving population with their share of friends and enemies.

The Algonquian

Shawnee neighbors and allies included the Delaware and the Miami who, like them, were Algonquian Indians, a group that also included the Fox, Sac, and Kickapoo tribes. The Algonquian, whose individual tribal languages are similar to one another, mostly occupied the Great Lakes region. The word *Shawnee* means "southerner" in Algonquian. Although the Shawnee were never a southern tribe in the strictest sense, the term "southerner" probably refers to the tribe's home in the Ohio River region, located at the south end of Algonquian territory.

Historians say that in 1700, twenty-seven years after Marquette and his part-ner Louis Jolliet first encountered the Shawnee, the tribe numbered about six thousand. The tribe had been organized into five separate divisions, each with its own specialty and function. For example, the Piqua division was concerned with spiritual matters, the Kispoko provided war chiefs, and the Mekoce oversaw medicine and health. The two most influential divisions were the Chillicothe and the Thawegila, as they provided the Shawnee nation with political leaders.

These five divisions were further broken down into twelve clans, each of which operated as an extended family. A clan was named after an animal: snake,

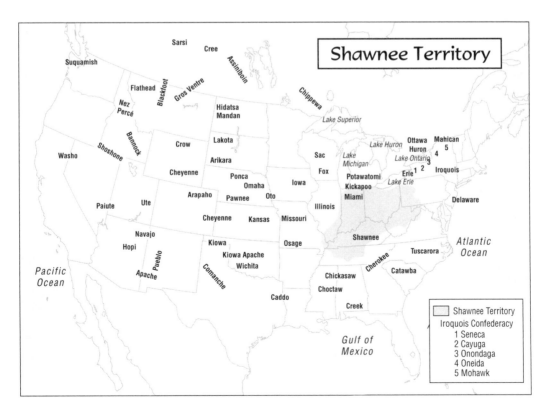

Shawnee Territory

Shawnee Territory
Iroquois Confederacy
1 Seneca
2 Cayuga
3 Onondaga
4 Oneida
5 Mohawk

A Shawnee belt celebrates the unity of the tribe. The Shawnee lived in clans named after different animals.

turtle, raccoon, turkey, hawk, deer, bear, wolf, lynx, elk, buffalo, and horse. Clan members were thought to exhibit characteristics associated with their clan animal. For example, Turtle women were expected to bear many children because female turtles lay many eggs. The five divisions and twelve clans survived the separations and migrations that the Shawnee experienced during their history.

The tribesmen who met Marquette and Jolliet were already under siege by the Iroquois, as that confederacy sought control of the lucrative Great Lakes fur trade; the two explorers even noted the Shawnee's plight in their journals. The tribe's subsequent departure from their home territory brought them in contact with Indian tribes who sometimes fought them, sometimes welcomed them, and sometimes even relied on them for protection.

Chapter 1

Wanderers and Warriors

The Shawnee's years on the move meant that they were frequently traveling through, or settling in, territory occupied by other Native Americans. Sometimes these tribes tolerated their presence, other times the Shawnee found themselves under attack. Yet exposure to new territories and cultures over a period of so many years may have given the Shawnee a unique level of sophistication. According to historian John Sugden, "The Shawnees [were] regularly uprooted and displaced. These constant [migrations] also resulted in . . . an exceptional knowledge of distant trails and waterways, and a broad perspective of the Indian predicament."1

Moreover, because of their frequent wanderings, the Shawnee became adept at moving. Their lifestyle could easily be reestablished in a new territory. And, as with other North American Indians, the Shawnee shaped their culture to fit the environment in which they lived. Even when they were not migrating, the tribe practiced a seminomadic lifestyle that suited the changing seasons of the central and eastern United States. During the summer months, when it was possible to grow corn and other crops, the Shawnee lived in permanent villages located on or near a river. Once the weather grew cold, villagers broke into small family groups and traveled, sometimes many miles, to winter camps, where they would live throughout the winter on whatever meat the men of the group could find.

Shawnee men took pride in being good hunters and warriors; indeed, their primary role was to feed and protect their families and fellow tribesmen. Other tribes developed a healthy respect for the Shawnee's fighting ability, which was undoubtedly honed through many years of migration. However, despite their warlike reputation, the Shawnee preferred to leave a territory to avoid trouble, rather than fight. As Sugden wrote,

Often the Shawnee did avoid confrontations, sometimes most strikingly by migrating. Rather than remaining in uncomfortable situations, whether they were the result of conflict, the proximity of irksome neighbors, or the poor hunting, the Shawnees were prone to removing, finding new homes where they could find their own inclinations unmolested.[2]

A desire for peace led the Shawnee to migrate out of the Ohio territory when warriors from the powerful Iroquois Confederacy of central New York took up arms against tribes in the Great Lakes region and Ohio.

A War over the Fur Trade

What historians call the Iroquois Confederacy is actually five separate New York tribes: the Cayuga, Mohawk, Oneida, Onondaga, and Seneca. They banded together as a defense against two large and powerful neighboring tribes, the Huron and the Erie.

The French fur traders and explorers who appeared in the St. Lawrence River region of New York in the sixteenth century had formed an alliance with the Huron, which greatly alarmed the Iroquois. The Huron and French collaborated on the region's lucrative fur trade. This was the start of what became known as the Beaver Wars. The Iroquois wanted their share in this trade, and by the 1630s decided to take it by force. At this point the confederacy had powerful European allies to help them—the Dutch and English, who were competing with France for resources

in the New World. Officials from both countries gave the Iroquois weapons and advice. The confederacy pushed hard against the Huron, their warriors moving southward through the Great Lakes region into Shawnee territory.

The Shawnee engaged in the fur trade but were not rivals to the Iroquois like the Huron were. Yet the settled and sophisticated Iroquois, farmers whose communities revolved around their longhouses, bore no love for the nomadic Shawnee. The confederacy would later warn the British, "[the Shawnee] are remarked for their deceit and perfidy, paying little or no regard to their word and most solemn engagements."[3] The British evidently ignored the advice since the Shawnee later became an ally of England.

The Iroquois, victorious in the Beaver Wars, proclaimed themselves stewards of the Ohio territory. They said all tribes that lived in that territory did so under their jurisdiction. The Shawnee, however, had already left the territory to escape the long conflict, and some historians say to also escape the spread of disease. Even as early as the seventeenth century, illnesses, such as smallpox, brought to North America by Europeans, had already caused significant deaths among Native American populations.

After the Beaver Wars

The entire Shawnee tribe had rarely, if ever, moved at the same time. Thus, after the Beaver Wars, different villages and divisions decamped at will, and the five

Who Were the Iroquois?

Longtime enemies of the Shawnee, the Iroquois were farmers, craftsmen, and warriors whose bark-covered long-houses were the center of community life. The original five nations, the Mohawk, Oneida, Seneca, Cayuga, and Onondaga, are thought to have come together as a confederation in the late sixteenth century to protect against powerful enemies in their home territory, New York. Europeans knew them simply as the League of Five Nations, or Five Nations. A sixth nation, the Tuscarora, was admitted in 1722.

Iroquois councils were fairly democratic, with delegates elected from clans within the Five Nations. Decisions for the entire Iroquois people usually required a unanimous vote of the league council. The Iroquois relied mostly on crops for food, primarily corn, but also pumpkins, beans, tobacco, apples, and peaches. They were known for their pottery, baskets, cornhusk mats, and wampum belts.

The Iroquois obtained European firearms fairly early in their history. This, along with their superior fighting ability, made the Iroquois particularly powerful during the colonial period of America. At the height of their influence, they controlled most of what is now the eastern United States: as far west as the Mississippi River and as far south as the Tennessee River.

Most Iroquois fought on the side of the British during the Revolutionary War, though the league council itself was neutral. After the war, the Mohawk and their leader Joseph Brant moved to Canada and were soon followed by the Cayuga. Today, most Iroquois live in New York, Ontario, and Quebec, though an Oneida group lives in Wisconsin and a Seneca-Cayuga group lives in Oklahoma.

Iroquois warriors fought on the side of the British during the Revolutionary War.

tribal divisions migrated in different directions. For example, members of the Chillicothe and Kispoko divisions moved south into Cherokee territory in eastern Tennessee. The Cherokee, however, were not unhappy to see them because the Iroquois were less likely to attack Cherokee villages with the Shawnee in the area. The Cherokee later allowed the Thawegila Shawnee to cross the Appalachian Mountains on their way to the Savannah River in South Carolina. This gesture was not so much altruistic as practical: By settling in South Carolina, the Shawnee would act as a protective buffer between the Cherokee

and the Catawba, a longtime enemy in the area. Most Piqua Shawnee traveled to southern Pennsylvania around 1677 and found refuge with their friends and allies, the Delaware. The remaining Piqua joined up with the Mekoce in Illinois, where they allied themselves with the Miami and Illinois Indians, who were also enemies of the Iroquois.

However, shifting tribal alliances and a shortage of animals to hunt kept the Shawnee on the move. Overcrowding in the Illinois territory led to overhunting, which meant that deer, rabbit, and other animals the people relied on for food had

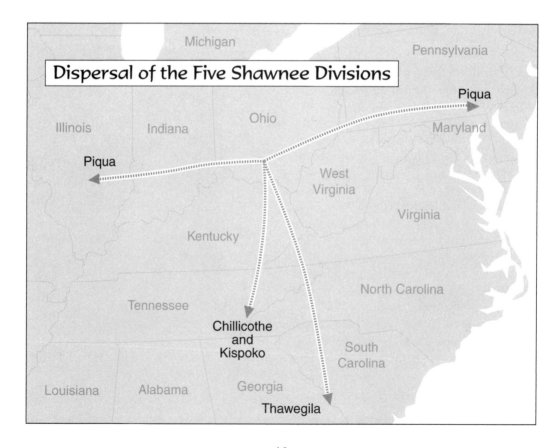

Dispersal of the Five Shawnee Divisions

become scarce. This led to a confrontation in 1689 between the Shawnee and the tribe the French explorers had named the Illinois. The Shawnee left the area to either join their relatives in Tennessee, or to travel to the Munsee and Mahican territories in northern Pennsylvania.

The relationship between the Shawnee and Cherokee soured in 1690 as more and more of the Illinois Shawnee settled in Tennessee. The two tribes began to clash, and after years of conflict, the Shawnee left Cherokee territory. By 1729, most had moved north to Kentucky and Ohio.

Meanwhile, the Pennsylvania Shawnee also found their new territory overcrowded and overhunted, particularly when European settlements began to appear. They, too, moved westward through Pennsylvania and, like their Tennessee brethren, returned to the Ohio River valley.

Home Again to the Ohio

There are many reasons why, after a century of separation, the various bands of Shawnee would regroup in the Ohio territory. By the beginning of the eighteenth century, the Beaver Wars had long since ended, and though the Iroquois still kept a presence in Ohio, they were no longer likely to attack the Shawnee, particularly since the latter's ally, the French, had established themselves there. Around the same time, the Shawnee's close allies, the Delaware, had invited them to settle in Delaware territory in Ohio. Meanwhile, the eastern United States, which by this time had

many white settlements, grew more and more crowded each year.

By 1758, the Shawnee nation, except for some members who had stayed in Creek Indian territory in Alabama, was living on the north side of the Ohio River valley in Ohio, between the Allegheny and Scioto Rivers. The land was lush and fertile, covered with trees and green river valleys. Of course, French and English traders were also living in the territory. British colonists had begun the move westward across the Appalachians to settle what was for them the western frontier. But for a time, at least, the Shawnee lived in relative peace, free to follow a way of life their ancestors had practiced before them: adapting to the seasons by hunting in the winter and farming in the summer.

Summer Villages and Winter Camps

The focus of every Shawnee community was the village where it would gather during the warm months to renew friendships, raise crops, play games, and celebrate traditional ceremonies. In the autumn, members of these villages would disperse to small winter camps scattered about the Shawnee territory.

A Shawnee village might contain more than one hundred homes, although certainly some villages were smaller. Most were built in river valleys where soil is fertile, and almost all were permanent. As long as no hostile tribes or white settlements appeared in the area, a village might remain for decades.

Shawnee summer homes were rectangular in shape, their walls and roofs made of bark. Whites who lived with or visited the Shawnee depicted these homes as being about twenty feet long and fourteen feet wide. As Christopher Gist, an early British explorer, described a Shawnee village in the seventeenth century, "[The village] contains about 300 men . . . there are about 40 houses on the south side of the river, about 100 on the north side, with a kind of state house of about 90 feet long, with a light cover of bark on it."[4]

The "state house" to which Gist referred was actually a Shawnee council house, the centerpiece of community life. These council houses were described as more than one hundred feet long, encompassing three rows of vertical posts, a pitched roof, cross beams, and planked walls. Fires burned in the center, while logs along the sidelines served as seats, as these very public buildings were used for tribal meeting places and ceremonies.

The council house, like the family homes around it, hummed with activity during the warm months. But when cold weather came, the close-knit village broke up into family groups. Each group pitched winter hunting camps, which were not

During the summer, the Shawnee lived in villages centered around a council house like this one. The council house was used for tribal meetings and ceremonies.

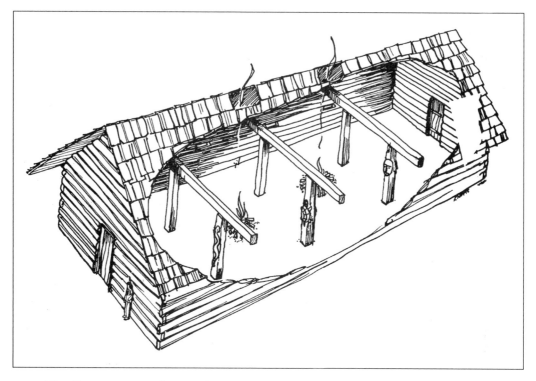

The Shawnee "state house" had fires burning in the center of the building with surrounding logs used as benches.

permanent since the Shawnee were careful not to overhunt a particular territory and would move on if game became scarce. The men hunted and trapped through the cold months, while the women processed the meat and tanned hides.

Winter-style homes were small, circular, and built with a pole foundation, with a place in the center for a fire. As historian Henry Harvey described, "[The Shawnee winter home] is made of small poles, the large ends of the poles are stuck in the ground and the small ends lashed together at the top. It is covered with animal skins so that the upper ones lap over the under ones. The fire is built in [the] center of the floor and the smoke goes out of the smoke hole left at the top."[5]

On the Road

Cold-weather homes were simple to make and easy to abandon, an important factor since the family would leave for their summer home in a few months. Whether migrating to new territory or going home to their village, the Shawnee always traveled light. They packed clothes, cooking utensils, buffalo robes, and blankets on the backs of their horses. Women would also carry some burdens themselves. O.M.

Spencer, who was captured by the Shawnee and lived with the tribe in 1792, pitied the Shawnee women and considered them beleaguered and overworked. As Spencer explained,

> I have often seen families traveling, and while the poor squaw, bending under the weight of a heavy load, and the girls, carrying packs or the smaller children on their shoulders, were laboring along, the lazy Indian in front might be seen with nothing but his rifle and blanket, and the boys with only bow and arrows. . . . [6]

However, as historians point out, the "lazy" Indian male had to be armed and alert lest enemy warriors should suddenly appear. Since the Shawnee often trekked through unfamiliar territory, they often did encounter hostile individuals or parties.

Shawnee males considered it a great honor to fight and die bravely; the art of war was something the tribe took very seriously. Once a war began, its participants observed traditions and ceremonies deeply rooted in Shawnee culture.

Declaring War

The Shawnee went to war for a number of reasons: to avenge a raid on their own village, to defend territory under attack, or to help a friendly tribe that had been attacked. War declaration was always accompanied by circulating a tomahawk painted in red clay among the various Shawnee villages, then among the villages of friendly Indians, such as the Delaware, who might send warriors to help the Shawnee cause.

All the warriors would gather in full war regalia in the village of the principal Shawnee war chief, who held a grand council of war. Shawnee war chiefs, traditionally members of the Kispoko clan, included some of the most illustrious names in Indian history: Cornstalk, Blue Jacket, Blackfish, and finally, Tecumseh. These warriors were known for their military tactics, intelligence, and courage in the face of overwhelming odds. For the Shawnee, excellence in warfare was a defining tribal trait.

Shawnee warriors prepared for battle by fasting and calling on guardian spirits for help. They would paint their bodies and festoon themselves with talismans, or charms, thought to have sacred properties that would protect them in battle. These talismans were mostly made from herbs, animal skins, and feathers—materials associated with the warriors' guardian spirits.

Before the battle, warriors formed a circle around what was known as a war post. They would take turns striking the post with their tomahawks and giving descriptions of their past glories in battle. The village hosted a war dance and warriors left singing a war song. These ceremonies were meant to raise morale and strengthen tribal unity.

The Shawnee rarely engaged in the kind of formal tactics used by Western armies.

Instead, the Shawnee relied on hit-and-run raids and ambush techniques, which could inflict damage on the enemy without many casualties on their side.

The Shawnee returned from battle noisily. Warriors whooped, displayed the scalps taken in battle, and, once they had acquired firearms, fired shot after shot into the air. If prisoners had been taken, they were brought back to the village to face their fate—a fate that could be quite benign, despite the tales told by whites who feared Indians and considered them savages.

A Captive's Story

Few white captives could tell as dramatic a story as Mary Draper Ingles, the Virginia woman captured by the Shawnee outside her home in July 1755. Ingles, then pregnant, and her two young sons were taken on a twenty-day trek to the Ohio River, outside of what is now Point Pleasant, West Virginia. Several days later they crossed the Ohio at the mouth of the Scioto River, heading north to the Shawnee village of Chillicothe. Along the trail, Mary had given birth to a daughter.

Mary's two boys, George and Thomas, were eventually adopted by a Shawnee chief who took them into his home. Mary, meanwhile, was living with, and working for, a pair of French traders who lived in the village. While on a salt-making expedition to an area known as Big Bone Lick, Mary and a fellow captive, a Dutch woman whose name is not recorded, escaped their captors. Knowing that her baby could never survive a long journey through the wilderness, and that the Indians would undoubtedly care for her, Mary left the child behind.

Mary and her companion followed the Ohio River upstream on its Kentucky side, surviving on nuts, berries, and insects. They traveled about eight hundred miles along the river and its tributaries to reach Mary's home territory. Both were near death, but ultimately survived. Mary's hair turned completely white and never returned to its former auburn color. She and her husband William were reunited and eventually had four more children. Upon searching for their children in Ohio, the Ingleses learned that George had died but that Thomas was being raised by the Shawnee. They eventually ransomed him back, but he never lost his love for the Shawnee people and their way of life.

The tribe was deeply impressed that Mary had survived her ordeal and arrived home safely. The remainder of Mary's life was fairly uneventful. She died in 1815 at the age of eighty-three. The baby daughter she had left behind was never located.

Captives of the Shawnee

As a rule, captives were adopted by the tribe, put to work in the village, or married to a Shawnee man or woman. Child captives, whether white, black, or Indian, were eagerly adopted by Shawnee families. Adoptive Shawnee were considered full members of the tribe and treated as such. White captives often became so fond of their Shawnee families that when help arrived they preferred to stay with the tribe rather than return with their rescuers. Christian missionary Joseph Rhodes, who lived for a time in Shawnee territory during the nineteenth century, told of a white woman who had willingly spent her life with the Shawnee. Rhodes said, "A white woman [in the village] that was taken prisoner whilst she was so young that she cannot speak a word of English and there is very little difference between her and the Shawnees that is the younger branches of the family." [7]

The Shawnee became equally fond of their prisoners. White adoptees and spouses could live for years with the tribe, siring or bearing children, and would think of the Shawnee as their "true" family. During an eighteenth-century prisoner exchange with the American colonists, Shawnee chief Lawoughgua said,

The Shawnee used weapons like the bow and arrow to hunt and in battle. To prepare for war, warriors would fast and call to the spirits for help.

The Shawnee as Mercenary

Shawnee warriors were so well regarded for their fighting ability that when bands of them migrated to a new territory, the Native Americans who lived there might encourage them to stay. For example, in the seventeenth century, the Cherokee allowed the Shawnee to remain in their territory so long as they acted as a buffer between Cherokee villages and war parties of the Catawba, the Cherokee's longtime rivals and enemies. Thus, the Shawnee and Catawba, who were well armed by nearby British settlements, fought often.

However, the Shawnee were most concerned with protecting their lands, hunting grounds, and people. If they needed to switch sides to defend their interests they would do so. For example, during the French and Indian War the Shawnee fought against the British, but in the Revolutionary War they allied with the British, all in hopes of defending their territory.

The Shawnee found themselves on the side of the Spanish in 1773 and 1779 when three of the five clans broke from the tribe and left for southeast Missouri, a Spanish territory. Spain hoped that the Shawnee would act as a line of defense against American settlers who might cross the Mississippi River into Spanish territory. Spain's emissaries even came to Ohio in 1788 to try to persuade more Shawnee and their close allies, the Delaware, to emigrate to Missouri. Some did, but most Shawnee elected to remain in Ohio until the Indian Removal Act forced them into Kansas in 1832.

We have taken as much care of these prisoners as if they were our own flesh and blood. . . . They are now unacquainted with your customs and manners, and therefore, Fathers, we request you will use them tenderly and kindly, which will be a means of inducing them to live contentedly.[8]

Even so, especially when emotions ran high after a battle, the Shawnee sometimes executed and tortured white prisoners. But such incidents were often exaggerated by whites who wished to make trouble for the Indians. Chief Black Hoof, one of the most renowned Shawnee leaders, told interviewers late in his life that decent-minded Shawnee disliked the torture of innocent people, especially women and children. Torturing women and children dishonored ancient traditions, he said.

However, torture and execution were not unheard of for captured combatants who were not considered "innocent," and for fighters of any race who had taken up arms against the Shawnee. Of all the punishments meted out to Shawnee captives, none was more famous than the gauntlet, an event which involved an entire village, including women, children, and the elderly.

A contemporary sketch of a Shawnee warrior. The Shawnee were known for their skill in battle.

Running the Gauntlet

There are several historical accounts of the Shawnee gauntlet, including one from Spencer's memoir of his captivity. A fellow prisoner of Spencer's, a man named Moore, was chosen to "run" the gauntlet. As Spencer said,

> Men, women and children invited from neighboring villages, flocked to the capital of the Shawnees. . . . Here, after gratifying their curiosity in examining the prisoner, armed with clubs, switches and other instruments of punishment, they arranged themselves facing each other in two rows about seven feet apart. . . . Moore was led out and stripped to the waist . . . starting a short distance from the head of the lines, he soon bounded through them. . . . So effectually did he use his feet, head and right wrist, hitting some, striking down others . . . [that] amid the shouts of the warriors he soon reached the goal. Having passed the ordinary trial he was congratulated as a brave man. [9]

Female captives, such as Mary Draper Ingles of Virginia, also reported running the gauntlet. Some of Ingles's white male contemporaries described the gauntlet as a kind of tribal hazing, or Shawnee initiation. But the gauntlet turned into a brutal experience if the prisoner tried to escape. As Ohio frontiersman Simon Kenton learned,

> Kenton was taken to [an Indian village] on the Mad River, was made to run the gauntlet on the banks of the river and they . . . beat him almost to death. . . . He knocked down [one of his tormentors] and plunged into the river and would have made his escape but for a horseman. He was captured and taken back with a broken arm for his trouble. [10]

A Warrior's Death

Captives who had somehow wronged the Shawnee were often publicly executed, in keeping with the Shawnee sense of justice. A white or Indian captive might be executed in retaliation for crimes he or his tribe or nation committed. Female tribal members who lost loved ones in a battle involving the prisoner might participate in the execution.

A prisoner undergoing a public execution would be shaved, painted, and tied to a post. The Shawnee captors would pile slow-burning wood at his feet, and before lighting it, might stone or slash him, or otherwise cut or mutilate him.

If, however, the Shawnee engaged in cruel practices, they also taught their sons that a warrior must die bravely. Were they to face a slow, painful death, they were expected to do so with dignity. Prisoners who died terrified served as examples of cowardice. Those who kept their dignity served as role models for other warriors.

War and Culture

The Shawnee believed that capture dishonored a warrior. But if he showed no fear at the time of death this dishonor was erased, and he went to the next world as a hero. A great warrior was also a great protector of one's people. And for the Shawnee, war was always a last resort to preserve the Shawnee way of life: its strong families, religious beliefs, moral codes, and cultural traditions.

Chapter 2

Becoming Shawnee

Every member of the Shawnee tribe had a role to play, and these roles were mostly divided between the sexes. Adult males hunted and trapped, and defended the tribe from its enemies. Adult women grew corn and other crops, gathered plants and herbs from the surrounding woodlands, cooked, made clothes, and cared for their homes and children. Boys and girls spent their growing up years learning how to do the tasks they would be expected to perform in adulthood: Even playtime and games might be a time to learn adult skills.

The work of both men and women was valued. Both sexes participated in tribal government and in Shawnee community and cultural life. The tribe expected its men *and* its women to play their roles well, since both were responsible for feeding the community and keeping its families safe. A Shawnee man, for example, would be held in low esteem if he was a poor hunter or a coward on the battlefield.

A Shawnee Hunt

A Shawnee hunt, particularly in the winter, could continue for days, with all able-bodied men joining the hunting party and tracking their quarry through the woods. Larger game included elk, deer, black bear, and buffalo, the latter of which was plentiful in the Midwest and eastern United States prior to European arrival. The hunting party would eat enough of its kill to make a meal, then take the rest back to camp. If they killed more meat than they could carry, they would hang the meat in trees, out of reach of predators, and return for it later.

In addition to bows and arrows, clubs, and, much later in Shawnee history, rifles, a hunter usually carried two staples with him on the hunt—a bag of corn-meal and a blanket. When game was scarce and nourishment necessary, the hunter could simply mix a handful of cornmeal with water and lap up the mush, while the blanket provided shelter and warmth.

In his book *History of the Shawnee Indians*, Harvey wrote, "A Shawnee is seldom without a blanket, it is used as a cover at night, and a wrapper by day. They use them while out hunting and as ceremonial dress. . . . The blanket is also used to wrap provisions." [11]

Lacking refrigeration, Shawnee women dried and dehydrated as much meat as possible, storing it in skins, hide, clay containers, or baskets. According to an account preserved in the Indian archives of the Oklahoma Historical Society, the Shawnee made use of the sun and the open air when they processed their meat. The account stated,

After returning from a hunt, [the Shawnee] would cut the meat into strips and place it on the roofs of their [houses] to dry. This was done at all seasons of the year, even summer. In the old days, the only flies were green flies. This was done with both buffalo and deer meat. [12]

Women's Work

In addition to preparing and storing meat, Shawnee women were also responsible for cultivating corn and other vegetables. The women planted corn by dropping seeds into holes they had poked in the soil with sticks. When the corn was about a foot high, they would add beans, pumpkins, and squashes to the garden. The Shawnee complemented the food they grew with the food they gathered: wild

To preserve meat, Shawnee women cut it into strips and hung it to dry. Women cared for the home, raised children, and harvested crops.

The Shawnee grew corn, beans, squash, and pumpkins. They gathered other foods to supplement the harvest.

plums and berries, crab apples, grapes, persimmons, and nuts and herbs, such as sassafras, onions, and mustard, which were used for seasoning. The Shawnee did not keep domestic animals, such as goats or sheep, but did fish the nearby streams and rivers for trout and bass. In the late winter and early spring, the women took on another task: sugar making. They would tap nearby maple trees for sap, boil that sap, and make sugar. Though they did not kill large game, women did hunt rabbit, waterfowl, and other small game animals that were plentiful in the summertime.

Corn remained the staple of the Shawnee diet, although the Indians could not store a tremendous amount of it over the winter. As Shawnee author Thomas Wildcat Alford said,

It took a great deal of ingenuity to keep a supply from one year's crop until another could be grown and harvested. The usual method was of stripping back the husks and shucks of the corn . . . and braiding them securely, in long ropes, with the ears dangling. These ropes were hung inside [the family home], high up against the roof, when the family had no other storehouse.[13]

Once harvested, the corn was pounded and kneaded and made into bread, or was boiled and roasted. Shawnee women also used corn husks to help prepare meats and fish. The usual methods for cooking meats and fish involved roasting over a fire or with the food wrapped in corn husks and placed in hot coals; steaming, using wet corn husks or mud; or baking.

The tasks of a Shawnee wife and mother went well beyond cultivating corn

Shawnee women wove baskets out of tree bark. Other containers were made out of gourds and dried clay.

and cooking meals. She kept the fires going throughout the day, cared for her children, created containers out of gourds and dried clay, and wove baskets from elm and hackberry tree bark. After peeling bark strips from tree trunks, a Shawnee woman could weave a basket so tight it could hold water, or so loose it could sift cornmeal.

Shawnee women took such pride in their homes that at least one captive made note of it. During his enforced stay in a Shawnee home in the late eighteenth century, O.M. Spencer interacted with a Shawnee family, ate meals with them, and observed their culture. About his hostess's housekeeping skills, Spencer said, "[The squaw] was remarkably nice with in her cookery, requiring her kettles to be scoured often and her bowls and spoons to be washed daily, and nothing offended her quicker than the appearance of [slovenliness]."[14]

But far more important to Shawnee women—and their husbands—was family. From the time of their birth, children were eagerly welcomed into Shawnee society.

Birth and Naming

When it came time for a Shawnee woman to bear a child, she went off by herself to a hollow or a clearing in the woods not far from her village or camp. She remained alone with the baby for several days, keeping shelter beneath the trees and building a fire to keep warm. Then she went home to her village, where the baby was admired by its father, family members, and friends.

Shawnee Grooming

Shawnee men and women cared about their looks and were particularly proud of their black hair. The men would dress their hair with bear fat to make it glossy, sometimes mixing in soot to make for an even darker shade. A common male hairstyle was to wear the sides short, with a high ridge of hair like a pompadour from the forehead to the back of the neck. Only warriors wore feathers, signifying they had killed enemies in battle.

Shawnee women grew their hair very long, and enjoyed gathering it into a thick mass that hung from the back of their heads and resembled a beaver tail. They often decorated this "beaver tail" with colorful wrappings. The women also combed bear fat through their hair to make it glossy.

Shawnee women kept their clothing simple. They wore a long rectangular piece of animal hide held in place by a belt, moccasins on their feet, and, at times, leggings. The men usually wore moccasins, leggings, and a breechcloth. During cold weather, the Shawnee draped their upper bodies and arms with fur robes, mantels, caps, and animal hides. Clothes for festive occasions might be decorated with dyed moose hair and porcupine quills woven into intricate patterns.

After prolonged contact with Europeans, many Shawnee adopted European-style clothing. They made clothes from wool and cotton rather than animal skin, and men wore trousers, shirts, and coats instead of leggings, robes, and mantels. Women wore cotton dresses, and used ribbons and beads, in lieu of quills and moose hair, as decorations for ceremonial costumes.

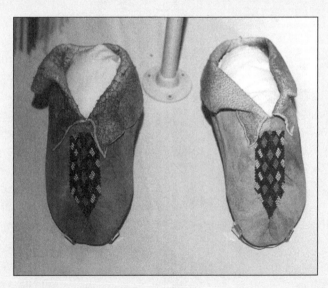

The Shawnee wore moccasins like these to protect their feet.

Shawnee girls learned a variety of skills from their mothers, such as how to mold clay pots like this one.

This practice suggests that Shawnee babies tended to be robust from birth. There were, however, exceptions.

According to Bil Gilbert, author of *God Gave Us This Country: Tekamthi and the First American Civil War*, "Occasionally a child with severe birth defects was abandoned but cases of this sort of infanticide were rare." [15]

Boy babies were named ten days after birth, girls twelve days. A tribal elder chose the name after examining the child and taking into consideration the circumstances of its birth and ancestry. Every Shawnee belonged to one of the twelve clans, and each clan was matrilineal. This meant that each Shawnee traced his or her lineage through his or her mother's clan. Thus, a Shawnee name usually derived from the mother's clan. Names also reflected the child's physical characteristics and could be changed as he or she grew and changed. In his book, Gilbert wrote, "If a child first called Swift Deer grew to be a chubby, heavy-footed little boy, this was recognized by changing his name to something on the order of Deer in the Snow." [16]

Shawnee mothers kept their babies with them at all times, on a cradle board known as a *tkithoway*, which was carried on the back. A *tkithoway* was carved from wood and decorated according to the parents' taste. Some writers believe that the device was used to keep a child's back straight and strong. However, the cradle board was also a form of protection: If left alone on the ground or on a blanket, an infant would be vulnerable to wild animals.

When able to walk, the Shawnee child began to participate in the activities of the family and tribe. Boys and girls lived a life filled with work and play.

Growing Up Shawnee

For Shawnee children, school was everyday life, and the world around them their classroom. From a very young age,

Shawnee children had to learn to control their emotions, since the survival of the group depended on it. For example, a young child's cry could frighten away an animal that the men were hunting for supper, or could help an enemy locate a band of travelers in the woods.

The Shawnee disliked gossip, dishonesty, and disrespect for one's elders. As Shawnee writer Thomas Wildcat Alford said,

> The greatest difference that I have found in the social life of the two races—Indians and white people—is the deference paid to age. In all our gatherings and in our home life, the older people "had the floor," so to speak. They were given the consideration and deference of the younger people, and their counsel was listened to with respect. [17]

However, a Shawnee childhood involved much more than moral and spiritual training. Like children everywhere, they played and enjoyed life, and did so in ways that helped them learn skills they would use later in adulthood. Shawnee girls played alongside their mothers, learning where one might gather berries and persimmons, or how to mold vessels of clay. Shawnee boys played war games and team games that developed their hunting and defensive skills. Alford described one such game that involved bows and arrows. He wrote,

> A hoop was made out [of] a wild grape-vine bent around until the ends met and lapped a little, and tied securely with strips of bark. The group of boys "chose sides" . . . [and] rolled the hoop along the ground towards the opposite party of boys, who shot at it with their bows and arrows. The boy whose arrow stuck into the [opening inside the hoop] was the winner. [18]

Historical accounts differ as to when boys were considered men, but most indicate that the late teens and early twenties was the threshold of manhood. For girls, womanhood was when they married and became mothers. Girls usually married while in their mid-teens, and all marriages were arranged between families.

A Family Union

Shawnee marriages tied families together and strengthened tribal bonds. The family that one married into had to be chosen carefully. For example, if a man was injured or wronged in some way, his relatives, including his in-laws, took revenge for him.

Usually, a young man's family made the first overtures. His parents would choose an appropriate wife for him, then approach her family with presents. If her parents considered the young man a good prospect, they accepted the gifts, and then responded with gifts of their own. Shawnee couples had no formal wedding ceremony, but a feast would be held to celebrate the couple's union, after which the couple would set up a home and begin their life together. Most Shawnee mar-

Shawnee Adoption

Shawnee families frequently adopted prisoners taken by the tribe, particularly if those prisoners were children. However, not every adoptee was a prisoner. Some came to live with the tribe after a death in or abandonment by their birth family. Individuals who lived with the tribe by choice might also be adopted.

The tribe was known to adopt whites, blacks, and Indians from other tribes. Often the adoptive family had lost a family member and would take a new member to fill that hole. Young captives in particular were eagerly adopted by Shawnee couples with few or no children. Having children was particularly important in the Shawnee society because a child cared for his or her parents in their old age. If a Shawnee child was orphaned, he or she would be adopted by a family member or family friend. The great chief Tecumseh and his brother, the Shawnee Prophet, were adopted by Blackfish, one of their father's friends. Stephen Ruddell, a white child captured by the Shawnee, was adopted by them, given the name Big Fish, and became an eventual friend of Tecumseh. One of the more famous adult adoptees in Shawnee history was Daniel Boone, who later escaped from the tribe.

Once adopted, the individual was considered to be a full member of the family and the Shawnee tribe. In 1761, the Shawnee conducted a prisoner exchange with the British involving hundreds of white prisoners. Roughly half of those prisoners refused to go with the British and remained with their Shawnee families.

riages occurred in summertime, when the community itself came back to life.

Polygamy, the practice in which a man takes more than one wife, was allowed, although it appears to have been rare. Historians theorize that polygamy occurred when the male population was smaller than normal, usually because a number of the men had died in battle. With fewer husbands to go around, some men would take another wife. The Shawnee also permitted divorce if the differences between spouses were very serious. Divorce could be initiated by either the man or the woman. For example, the fellow tribesmen of the wife of a poor hunter and provider would deem it acceptable for her to leave and find a new husband. Or, if the wife were a poor mother to their children, her husband could order her out of their home and take a new wife to care for his children properly.

Festivals and Foot Races

Europeans who visited the Shawnee in the eighteenth century described their mid-summer season as near idyllic. Corn planting was finished at this point, berries ripened, and smaller game, such as rabbit and birds, was plentiful. Summer was also a time for family, clan and tribal gatherings, festivals, foot races, and games.

Gilbert, who wrote a detailed description of Shawnee culture in his Tecumseh biography, described the Shawnee as competitive sportsmen who loved to engage in organized events. The tribe often played a ball game very similar to modern-day lacrosse. Teams of men would play teams of women, or a team from one Shawnee village might play a team from another. These games, which continued from dusk to dawn for several days, were not unlike some of today's sporting events.

The Shawnee's love of fun offended some of their more conservative visitors, including the Reverend David Jones, who in the eighteenth century was the first European missionary to visit them. In an account of his visits to the Shawnee, he described a people who enjoyed life late into the night, visiting neighbors, dancing, playing games, gambling, and engaging in

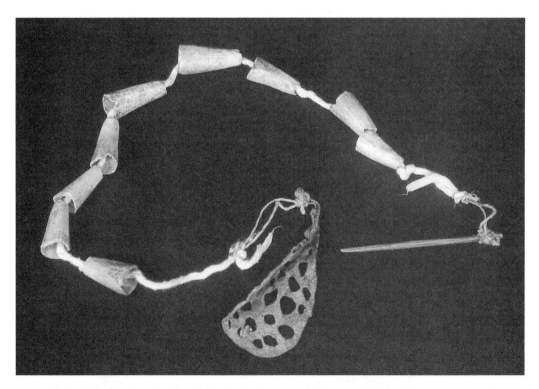

Pictured is a string used in a ring-and-pin game. In the summer the Shawnee engaged in many games and races.

The Bread Dance, a Shawnee Tradition

The Bread Dance, known as *Takuwhaw-nagaway* in Shawnee, was one of the tribe's most important religious and cultural rites. One dance was held in the spring during planting season, and the other in the fall, at harvest time. The Shawnee believed that before they planted corn, which was used to make bread, they should hold a Bread Dance, and one of their gods would bless the people and give them a good crop. The fall Bread Dance gave thanks for the crop and prayed for a good hunting season.

The Bread Dance had two committees of twelve men and twelve women apiece. The men hunted game—deer, wild turkey, quail, grouse, or squirrel—for the feast accompanying the dance. The committee of women baked bread and prepared the game the men would bring home. A tribal member well versed in the customs of the dance gave a blessing appropriate to the season. A ball game was played between the men and the women, then they participated in some initial dancing, doing a call-and-response chant meant to demonstrate the "rivalry" between the sexes. Whichever side lost the ball game had to gather wood for the bonfire. In the late afternoon, meat and bread were given to all.

The Shawnee believed that a happy, cheerful attitude gained the Great Spirit's favor, so joy and happiness were always expressed. The dance held after the feast included other members of the tribe and lasted all night, until sunrise.

practical jokes. He even described an incident when he was "beset by a band of strolling [Shawnee revelers], dressed in outlandish animal costumes." At first he was badly frightened, mistaking the masqueraders for a troupe of devil worshippers. "It appears," Jones observed reprovingly, "as if some kind of drollery was their chief study."[19]

But the Shawnee summer did have its serious side. Since the tribe grew its crops during warm weather, and much of the tribe's religious beliefs centered around agriculture, summer was also the time when the Shawnee practiced their most important rituals and traditions. The tribe held two dances, accompanied by feasts, known as "bread dances," one in the spring and one in the fall. The Green Corn Dance took place during the time the corn ripened. The spring Bread Dance, held when the corn was planted, asked the spirits to ensure a successful growing season. The autumn Bread Dance, held at harvest time, thanked the spirits for a good crop.

Chiefs for War and Peace

The Shawnee clung hard to their traditions, even as the tribe's contact with whites increased. They also continued their traditional style of sophisticated tribal government.

Of the tribe and its governing body, the missionary David Jones, who made two visits to the Shawnee, wrote,

> They are strangers to civil power and authority, they look on it that God made them free—that one man has no natural right to rule over another. . . . Every town has his head-men, some of which are called by us kings. . . . The chief use of these head-men is to give council, especially in time of war, they are used also as most proper to speak with us on any occasion. [20]

But like many Europeans, Jones misunderstood his American hosts. While it was true the Shawnee had a love of freedom, their leaders were not kings, and the scope of their chiefs' duties went far beyond talking to white men and giving advice at wartime.

Each Shawnee village had four chiefs, two for war and two for peace. The Shawnee nation was organized much the same way. Thus, four primary chiefs had charge of the entire Shawnee nation, and were advised by the four chiefs of the individual villages. However, historians point out that because the five divisions spent so much time away from each other, each one probably operated as an autonomous unit at some point in the nation's history. When the Shawnee came together again in Ohio in the eighteenth century, the nation remained loosely organized.

Shawnee chiefs had many duties. Four chiefs were assigned to each village, two for war and two for peace.

The principal peace chief of the village was a man, but his counterpart was female, and she might be a relative or his wife. The male peace chief handled disputes among tribal members and ran the tribe much as a mayor runs a city today. The female peace chief made certain that the planting and harvesting of crops went smoothly, and she oversaw the scheduling and cooking of feasts.

The male war chief directed all war efforts and took control of the village if war was declared. The female war chief, usually his wife, took care of war's practicalities, such as making sure that warriors and their families had enough to eat. In matters of war, the Shawnee system had a set of checks and balances. While the war chief directed the war, only the peace chief could declare war, or order the conflict to end if he deemed it necessary.

The war chief assumed his position because of past deeds. The position of peace chief was not inherited, but the chief's son could assume the same position if the tribal elders decided he was of good character. If a chief had no son, the elders of the tribe simply chose the best candidate. Each chief had help from his set of councillors. According to historian C.C. Trowbridge, "The aged men . . . sit behind the chiefs and when necessary they explain the proceedings at any previous council and generally afford their advice and assistance in the proceedings."[21]

The peace chief and his tribal council dispensed Shawnee justice. The tribe kept strict standards for its members. Thievery was not tolerated—anyone caught stealing was banished from the tribe. Gossip, another serious offense, could be punished by death. The penalty for murdering another tribal member could be death or paying tribute to the victim's family. The Shawnee who killed a fellow tribesman with a wife and children could be ordered to provide for them from then on.

The Shawnee believed that if revenge for a murder were not taken, the soul of the victim could not make its journey to the afterworld. The afterworld was of great concern to the Shawnee, since they believed the soul was immortal.

Chapter 3

Spirits and Shamans

Every facet of Shawnee existence—from birth to death, from hunting to harvests—had a spiritual component. The Shawnee believed that every living thing on the earth was inhabited by a spirit under the protection of a deity known as the Great Spirit, or *Kohkumthena*, meaning "our Grandmother" in the Shawnee language.

Traditional Shawnee spirituality encompasses rituals, sacred objects, faith, and ceremonies. Over the years the Shawnee have done their best to shield the details of their religion from white scrutiny. Even today, some Shawnee religious traditions and practices remain a well-guarded mystery.

Shawnee religious beliefs have a good deal in common with those held by other ancient cultures. The tribe believes that they are favored by the Great Spirit, and that the creation of the earth and all things in it was accomplished by two supreme beings, the Great Spirit and a male creator deity.

Chosen People

The Shawnee male deity is a remote, impersonal being who, tribal members believed, created the foundation for the earth by descending from a void and making the base upon which the earth rests—the back of a giant turtle. He then created the earth, placed it atop the turtle, and created animals and people to fill it. He also created Grandmother, whom the Shawnee also call the Great Spirit, and her companions, a little dog and her two grandsons. One of these grandsons caused such mischief that the male supreme being sent a flood upon the earth. All living things were destroyed by that flood, save for the Shawnee.

The Shawnee believe themselves to be the "chosen" people of Grandmother, who saved them from the flood. According to the Shawnee, Grandmother sent them a large white swan. These first Shawnee crawled atop the swan's back to wait out the flood. Then Grandmother sent down a great crayfish, who burrowed into the earth to drain it.

The male deity then allowed Grandmother to repopulate the world with living things. Once finished, Grandmother and her dog retired to her heavenly home. She then set upon weaving a great net which her dog unraveled every night. The Shawnee believed that when the net was finished the world would come to an end. At that time, Grandmother would lower this net to the earth, and all those who had proven themselves worthy would climb in the net, to be gathered up to the heavens. Those left behind would suffer a horrible fate.

Grandmother did not keep a direct hand in human affairs. Rather, she would impart information, such as news of future events, to her chosen people via prophets, who contacted Grandmother while in a trance. In addition, many smaller, lesser beings, known as spirits, were said to live on Earth, interacting with human beings.

The White Ghosts of Kentucky

It was 1773, and British emissary Thomas Bullitt was to meet with Shawnee chief Blackfish on behalf of Lord Dunmore, governor of the Virginia territory. Dunmore had sent him to negotiate a peace treaty for Kentucky settlements located just south of the Ohio River, in Shawnee hunting territory. Virginians and other white easterner settlers had been flocking to this land that Indians called *Can-tuc-kee;* the appearance of settlers in *Can-tuc-kee* had led to a series of ongoing raids by the Shawnee. Bullitt did not return with the treaty Dunmore wanted, but he did bring back an intriguing story. According to Bullitt, Blackfish claimed not to have the power to negotiate for *Can-tuc-kee*, nor could he grant white settlement in it. The land was Shawnee hunting ground, but it did not "belong" to them, he said. Rather, it belonged to the ghosts of the Azgens, a white people from the eastern sea who once lived there. The Shawnee killed off these white neighbors long ago, but their spirits still held sway over *Can-tuc-kee*, demanding respect from all who went there, Blackfish said.

Bullitt's tale is intriguing, particularly in light of speculation, and new evidence, that northern white explorers predated Columbus in the New World by many centuries. Other British explorers brought back stories of light-skinned Indian tribes who spoke Welsh, the national language of Wales. And, in Indiana, a group of Indians reported that their ancestors had fought against white warriors who left behind a suit of armor.

Alas, no trace of the armor, or the Azgens, has been found. But both stories have remained as colorful tidbits of frontier folklore.

A Shaking Tent was used by the shaman to communicate with spirits. The tent would shake while a shaman communed with spirit animals.

The most important spirits of all involved the harvest and the hunt. The tribe used agricultural ceremonies and dances to give thanks each growing season for a good harvest and planting. A good harvest meant that the spirits were pleased with the tribe. If they were displeased, the harvest would fail or perhaps an illness would fall on the tribe. When an animal was killed for its meat, the hunter asked the animal's spirit for forgiveness for taking its life.

Holy men or women called shamans, similar to priests in other cultures, were responsible for communicating with the spirits of the natural world, through ceremonies and rituals, few of which have been discussed with whites. Shamans were also responsible for tribal medicine and healing, although Shawnee wives and mothers also availed themselves of lifesaving skills.

Communicating with Spirits

Descriptions of actual Shawnee shaman rituals are rare, though one research report in the Oklahoma Historical Society

Archives tells of a ceremony known as the Shaking Tent, intended to facilitate communication between a shaman and the spirit world. The shaman built a cylindrical structure, or tent, some twelve feet high, entered the tent, and began singing a magical song. Soon the tent began to shake, and witnesses said they heard the voices of spirit animals conferring with the shaman, passing along cures for diseases and pinpointing the whereabouts of missing items or people.

Other means of communing with spirits were not so dramatic. Tobacco, for example, was thought to be a spiritually powerful item. The Shawnee placed a plug of tobacco in the *colas*, or flames, of a campfire and the petitioner made a prayer, confident that smoke from the burning tobacco carried the prayer to the Great Spirit.

Magic songs, dances, and words also carried weight with the spirit world. The Shawnee believed, for example, that the right magic words could make a deer stop in its tracks so that it could be killed. Cooperation from the spirits was so important that each boy, once he reached puberty, sought out a spirit helper, or guardian spirit, to help him through life. When a boy was twelve or thirteen years

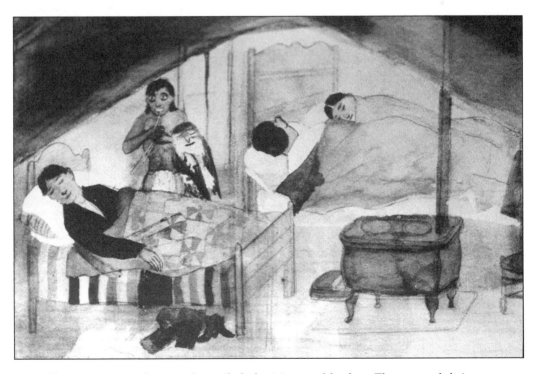

Shawnee women often acted as tribal physicians and healers. They created their own medicines from wild plants and herbs.

old, he went in the woods to fast and wait for a spirit helper to contact him. After a period of fasting and prayer the youth would sense the presence of a guardian spirit in the form of a bird or animal. During the encounter the spirit usually gave the youth some sort of instruction, or told him how to procure a talisman associated with the spirit to wear always. The youth came away from the encounter with practical knowledge as well, such as a healing method that could be put to use in daily life, and the awareness that he could count on the spirit for help in the future if contacted the proper way.

Healing Rites

The Shawnee, both past and present, have jealously guarded the identities of their herbs and medicinal plants. However, whites who lived with the Shawnee did record some of these rituals for posterity. Thus, it is known that the Shawnee boiled pumpkin pulp and bear oil together, then drank it to treat an upset stomach. An explorer who visited the tribe in winter described a successful Shawnee remedy for frostbite: Pound sassafras root into a powder, boil the powder in water until it forms a paste, then apply the paste to the frostbitten limb.

The Shawnee believed that healing powers came from the spirit world. The tribe closely guarded the identity of healing herbs and medicinal plants.

Spencer, during his captivity, developed dysentery and swollen feet. Of how a Shawnee woman treated him for these conditions, he wrote, "[She boiled] wild cherry bark and dewberry root, of which I drank frequently, and in which I occasionally soaked my feet for several days. She effected in a short time a perfect cure." [22]

Shawnee women frequently played the role of tribal physician and healer. Recalling his own mother's care and skill in setting his broken arm, Alford wrote,

> She took a limb about the size of my arm from an elm tree. Then she very dexterously slipped the bark from the limb and placed it bout my broken arm. She pulled the bone into place, adjusted it carefully and bound the bark comfortably loose about it. . . . I was kept quiet, given plenty of cold water until the fever had passed, and in due time my arm was perfectly healed. [23]

In accordance with their belief that all manner of healing emanated from the good will of the spirit world, the Shawnee did their best to stay on good terms with that world. Shawnee often kept spiritually powerful items with them, such as the feather or fur talismans that the men brought to a battle or hunt. For the tribe as a whole, though, no object was more sacred than the *Mishaami*, or sacred bundles.

Sacred Secrets

Each of the five Shawnee divisions had a sacred bundle, or *Mishaami*, the contents of which were said to have come from Grandmother herself. The bundles' contents were a closely guarded secret; very little is known about them even today. The Shawnee believed that even speaking about these bundles was sacrilegious. If the bundles still exist, their whereabouts are unknown to scholars.

The Shawnee believed the bundles had the power to protect the tribe from harm. In each division, a Shawnee of high character kept the sacred bundle safe: If anything happened to it, great harm could follow. Though information is sketchy, the bundles are believed to have been kept in a separate hut and guarded by their caretakers. Historians theorize that only two clans within each division were allowed to take charge of the bundle while it was being moved. During peacetime, a Turtle clan member carried the bundle because its clan's namesake animal moves slowly and with sure feet. In times of danger or flight, Turkey clansmen took charge of the bundle because turkeys were always ready to fly quickly. The *Mishaami* usually were transported onto the battlefield, because, it was believed, they made warriors powerful and increased the chance of success.

Only Grandmother could add or remove an item from a bundle. If she wished to make a change, she would communicate those wishes to a prophet, who could be male or female, and even a person of ordinary status.

Visiting the Heavens

Tenkswatawa, the most famous of the Shawnee prophets and brother of famed chief Tecumseh, changed his life after experiencing a prophetic vision. Tenkswatawa had been known as a poor hunter and problem drinker prior to a dramatic spiritual transformation. As Gilbert in his book *God Gave Us This Country* described,

> [He] collapsed and fell to the floor in a coma. . . . [His family] watched him through the night . . . it was decided

Tenkswatawa was known for his prophetic vision. He urged the Shawnee to cease imitating the ways of the European settlers.

A Solar Eclipse and an Earthquake

Both Tenkswatawa and his brother, the great Shawnee chief Tecumseh, were known for their gifts of prophecy, although Tecumseh is remembered more for his leadership than his visions. The most famous of Tenkswatawa's prophecies involved a solar eclipse. He had prophesied that the sun would turn dark, and his followers watched in astonishment as it did. White observers later wondered if Tenkswatawa had not consulted an English almanac in order to make his prediction.

Tecumseh made a very famous prediction during a visit to the Creek Indians of Alabama in 1811. He was seeking their support in his quest, beginning in 1808, to form an Indian confederation. When their meeting ended badly, Tecumseh told the Creek chief he was going straight to Detroit. Once there, he would stamp his foot and shake the ground in the Creek village, until all Creek homes came crashing down. Tecumseh left and the Creeks waited, counting the days when Tecumseh would presumably arrive in Detroit. On the very day they figured he would arrive, the ground did indeed begin to shake, and nearly all houses in the village collapsed. This incident is now known as the New Madrid, Mississippi, Earthquake, as this quake reverberated in the Mississippi River region. However, the Creeks saw it as a battle cry, and many of their warriors began to prepare themselves to help Tecumseh.

The spectacular confirmation of the earthquake notwithstanding, the projected confederation was short-lived. Tecumseh would later predict, on the eve of the War of 1812, that he would not survive the war. Tecumseh died on the battlefield in 1813.

Tenkswatawa's most famous vision foretold the occurrence of a solar eclipse.

that he was dead and funeral preparations were commenced. . . . Whereupon [Tenkswatawa] stirred . . . and said that he had undergone an experience similar to but more extraordinary than death. His soul had been taken from his body and presented to the Master of Life who . . . had told [him] what red people must do to . . . better themselves.[24]

Prior to the vision, Tecumseh's brother had been known as Lalawethika, the Rattle or Rattler. But afterwards he became known as Tenkswatawa, the Open Door; he was also known as the Prophet. He had brought back important information from Grandmother, he said. Indians must stop wearing European-style clothing made from wool and cotton. They should stop hunting with guns and making fire using white man's flint.

Tenkswatawa's experience was typical in that the Shawnee believed prophets could enter a trance state in which the soul traveled to Grandmother's home in the heavens. The prophet and Grandmother would confer, and she would impart the wisdom she wanted her chosen ones, the Shawnee, to learn. The people would hear Grandmother's message when the prophet awoke.

The Shawnee took Tenkswatawa's experience seriously, as they did all prophetic visions. Such conferences with Grandmother were the sole contact that the Shawnee would have with her other than death, after which one traveled permanently to the heavens. Since the Shawnee considered the human soul immortal, the afterlife was very important to them. Individuals had to prepare for death privately, but they could rely on their loved ones to see that they had a proper funeral.

Burial

Shawnee burial rituals were solemn, lengthy, and ultimately life affirming. According to historians, for about a half day after death, the body of the deceased person was kept inside the family home, where it was bathed, dressed in new clothes, and lain with its arms crossed over the chest. The body was removed from the home feet first, and any tracks left by those who had transported it were erased by sweeping the ground.

The deceased's family handled the four-day funeral, under the direction of a leader, usually a man. Two or three grave diggers were chosen, as well as women to cook the funeral feast. This funeral "team" faced a host of restrictions. They must not change their clothing, paint their faces or bodies, or wash their hair during the four-day period. The grave diggers were also forbidden to touch children, and they ate their food separate from the rest of the mourners.

After the body had been placed in a four-foot-deep, bark-lined grave, usually the day after death, the relatives would walk around it, always looking ahead; glancing backwards would have been an insult to the deceased.

The funeral leader delivered a funeral address, speaking about the deceased's life and accomplishments. This speech

A Shawnee Witch-Hunt

The Shawnee believed that spiritual power, which they called medicine, could be used for good or evil. For example, a purveyor of bad medicine, known as a witch, was credited with the ability to make an individual fall ill. Indians feared witches, and in 1806 the Delaware, with the help of the Shawnee Prophet, attempted to expose as witches persons they believed had made an entire village sick.

The Delaware communities along the White River were experiencing a rash of illnesses and misfortune. Tenkswatawa was called to help them purge "witchcraft" from their villages. Historians point out, in fairness to Tenkswatawa, that he did not instigate the witch-hunt. The Delaware appeared to have chosen the "witches" ahead of time, and may have had ulterior motives in doing so. Before Tenkswatawa arrived, one of the alleged victims was tortured until he admitted to the tribe that he held evil tokens. The man was subsequently tomahawked and burned. Another accused witch, a woman, was roasted over a slow fire after Tenkswatawa arrived. A Mohican Christian who served as an interpreter between the whites and the Delaware was clubbed and burned. Two Christian Delaware, both subchiefs, were burned at the stake. According to one historical account, some of these individuals had been blamed for conceding land to whites, against the wishes of the tribe.

Any connection between these individuals and the misfortune they were accused of having perpetrated is, of course, impossible to prove.

The inquisition finally ended when the brother of an accused intervened. The woman had been tied to the stake when her brother walked through the crowd and freed her. No other burnings or incidents of torture occurred after she was freed. However, some whites on the frontier heard of the witch-hunt and put all the blame on Tenkswatawa.

The Shawnee believed that prophets could use their spiritual power for both good and evil.

was followed by a large funeral feast, though one mourner always took care to keep the fire lit at graveside three days in a row. The Shawnee believed that this fire lighted the way for the spirit's journey to the heavens.

However, they believed that the spirit did not leave for heaven immediately. It lingered after death, and on the third night, the mourners would gather for a final farewell. They would light fires at the family home and gather for an all-night vigil. Another meal, called "eating the last meal with the dead," was served. The tribal elders told myths and tales through the night. The spouse of the deceased sat all night among the home fires. In the morning, the Shawnee believed the spirit left Earth to go to heaven, traveling westward to the edge of the world, the horizon, where it found a pathway to Grandmother's realm.

Life Goes On

On the fourth morning, the mourners underwent a purification ceremony that included head washing, and afterwards the house was swept, the old fires extinguished, and new fires lit. A final meal ended the funeral ceremony.

The spouse, in particular, underwent head washing and face painting, donning new clothes supplied by the deceased's birth family. A new mate could be chosen at this time, and if the spouse was a woman, she was especially encouraged to take a husband for the sake of her children and herself. If the prospective spouse had attended the funeral, she could select him once the ceremonies ended. The mourners would then leave, and the two of them would set up their home together. If she did not select a spouse, she would go home with her blood relatives and the responsibilities of her husband's family would end.

The dead were never forgotten. Tribal members were honored after their deaths. If a particularly distinguished person passed away, a special ceremony, known as the Turning Dance, was held a year later.

Dance for the Dead

The Turning Dance was performed over a four-day period, like the mourning ceremony. Men and women danced each of the four days, starting at noon. As with most Shawnee ceremonies, the Turning Dance was a chance for families and communities to reconnect with one another. The families and friends of the deceased made a point of collecting a large amount of food and goods, which would be divided up and contested for once the dance ended. For example, guests might compete over this cache by playing tug-of-war.

Researchers who have studied Algonquian tribes say that Shawnee burial rites and ceremonies are very similar to those practiced by fellow Algonquian. Historians also believe that some Christian beliefs influenced Shawnee religious practices. Like other tribes, the Shawnee encountered European missionaries and the beliefs they preached as early as the seventeenth century. Unlike some Native American tribes, however, the Shawnee resisted most efforts to convert them to Christianity.

Christianity's Influence

David Jones, the British missionary, found himself well received during his first visit to the tribe in 1772. However, he was pointedly told by the Shawnee not to speak his Christian beliefs in their villages. In his journals, Jones described how Chief Yellow Hawk, one of his hosts, had justified this request. Jones wrote,

> When God who first made us all prescribed our way of living he allowed white people to live one way and Indians another way; and as he was one of the chiefs of this town he did not desire to hear me on the subject of religion, for he was resolved not to believe what might be said or pay any regard to it. And he believed it would be the mind of other Indians.[25]

The Shawnee resistance to Christianity, which continued in the eighteenth and nineteenth centuries, may well have contributed to the preservation of the tribe's ancient traditions, cultural and religious.

But those who study tribal history believe Christianity may have had some impact on Shawnee religious beliefs. European explorers who chronicled the tribe spoke of an "Indian hell," similar to the place of punishment described in Christian literature. Fires and torments were believed to greet all who went to hell, Christian or Indian. However, there was a significant difference: Once a Shawnee had paid for the wrongs he or she had committed, he or she went to the abode of Grandmother and spent the rest of eternity in peace.

Others point to a Christian influence in the lifestyle led by the Shawnee Prophet, Tenkswatawa, and his followers. Prophet's followers prayed with the help of a string of beans, considered a holy object; some historians compare these strings to the Catholic rosary. Followers were also encouraged to confess any evil acts they committed, which historians see as having been borrowed from the Wyandots, a neighboring tribe who had seen many of its members convert to Roman Catholicism.

Whether or not Christianity influenced the Shawnee, the tribe did resist any full-scale conversion to the faith. Although today's Shawnee practice Christianity and other Western religions, many do adhere to Shawnee beliefs, whether in tandem with Western religions or on their own.

Nineteenth-century missionaries like Joseph Rhodes made few if any converts. Rhodes did, however, come away with a good opinion of the tribe. According to Rhodes,

> [The Shawnee] appear to be as sociable and as civil as those that are willing to be called refined Christians and I think more so to their honour be it spoken and the white people shame. I

have never heard but one word like swearing since I have been here, which is going on three months and that one was to mock the whites.[26]

Unfortunately, most nonmissionary Europeans who preceded and followed Rhodes did not share his views. Those who traveled to Shawnee country saw it as a place they could, and should, possess, and the Native Americans a culture to be pushed aside and changed. The ensuing struggle between the Shawnee and whites threatened their livelihood and culture, and their very existence.

Chapter 4

Homecoming and Loss

During the 1700s, after years of migration, the five divisions of the Shawnee returned to their former territory in the Ohio River region. Their old enemy, the Iroquois, no longer threatened them, but a new opponent, white settlers and armies, awaited.

These newly returned Shawnee would ally themselves with whites during several European-induced conflicts. But they switched sides when it appeared their former enemy, Great Britain, might help them rid their lands of both white settlers and white influence. The tribe fought alongside Great Britain during the Revolutionary War, and again in the War of 1812. These years were also filled with numerous conflicts between the Shawnee and the American settlers who spilled into Indian territory on the Ohio frontier. Conflicts with whites led to the first serious split in the Shawnee nation, one that altered the destiny of the tribe. Three of the five tribal divisions, unwilling to fight what they regarded as too-formidable an

enemy, broke away from the Shawnee nation and moved west to Missouri, then a property of Spain. Only the Mekoce and Chillicothe decided to stay and fight the battle that they would ultimately lose.

The history of conflict between Europeans and the Shawnee, particularly before the rise of Tecumseh, was a long and complicated one. A good way to study it is to divide it into three periods: early contacts and conflicts, which involved the fur trade, French traders, and the French and Indian War; clashes with American colonists and the alliance with Great Britain during the Revolutionary War; and the long series of skirmishes and battles with settlers, armies, and the American government that culminated in the Shawnee's defeat at the Battle of Fallen Timbers.

The tribe's first contacts with whites were economic, not violent, though doing business with Europeans would change the Shawnee in ways that no one, least of all the Indians themselves, would foresee.

A Business in Fur and Hides

The English and French traders who came to do business with the Shawnee in the seventeenth and eighteenth centuries were, for the most part, treated quite well. According to this account of Gist's 1750 encounter with the tribe, "The Lower [Shawnee] Town, just below the mouth of the Scioto, and the large Indian town of Piqua were visited. Gist distributed presents and received, in return, renewed pledges of friendship on the part of the Indians." [27]

These European traders often fit in quite well with the tribe. Most of them did not come to the territory to take their land or change their culture. Many married Shawnee women, fathered children with them, and kept permanent homes in Shawnee villages. Nonetheless, even these Europeans made a significant impact on Shawnee culture.

Fur traders, for example, were interested in an animal's hide, not its meat. In order to provide the traders with the fur and skins they wanted, the Shawnee began to kill animals they had never hunted before, such as lynx. The Shawnee also did a huge trade in deerskin, killing more deer in a hunt than would normally be killed for food.

Not surprisingly, the European demand for fur and hides led the Shawnee to hunt harder and farther afield, causing game to become scarce in some areas.

Other Forces for Change

The items the Shawnee received in trade for furs changed their lives and the way they did things. Men and women began to wear clothing made not from animal skin, but from cotton, wool, and other European fabrics. They also started to wear silver jewelry obtained in trade with the Euro-

After Europeans settled in the region, the Shawnee began to wear more European fashions.

peans. Men carried guns and knives instead of bows and arrows. Shawnee women began to serve foods not native to their region. When Jones arrived in Shawnee country some twenty years after the explorer Gist, he was served chocolate as part of his morning meal. Jones's hosts had undoubtedly obtained the chocolate from one of the many traders who passed through their village. (Chocolate is made from the cacao bean, a plant not grown in North America.)

By the time O.M. Spencer met Blue Jacket, a great war chief, in 1793, white clothing was so preferred that even Blue Jacket, a fierce opponent of white expansion, was dressed like a British nobleman in moccasins. According to Spencer,

> [Blue Jacket] was dressed in a scarlet frock coat, richly laced with gold and confined around his waist with a party-colored sash, and in red leggings and moccasins . . . on his shoulders he wore a pair of gold epaulets, and on his arms broad silver bracelets, while from his neck hung a massive silver gorget and a large medallion of His Majesty, George III.[28]

The Shawnee undoubtedly enjoyed these new weapons, tools, and clothing, but whether they knew it or not, these "riches" had changed their culture. As Sugden wrote, "The fur trade enriched the material culture of the Shawnee. [But] the fur trade was encouraging a new kind of Shawnee, an individualist who accumulated property in the style of the whites and whose home reflected a fatter living."[29]

The demand for guns and other goods made the Shawnee, and other Indians, increasingly dependent on white traders. Moreover, the overhunting of their territory reduced the amount of available game. The Shawnee would come to depend more on European goods for food.

As British traders displaced the French, the business of fur trading itself changed. More often than not French traders had simply passed out trade goods, with or without furs, to win loyalty of the tribe. The British, however, insisted on trade and trade only. Always an egalitarian people, the Shawnee became more interested in possession. However, they might have gone on to live in peace, their culture mostly undisturbed, had Europeans not decided to settle the North American continent, and in large numbers.

The French and Indian War

During the seventeenth century and through much of the eighteenth, Euro-American settlers concentrated their efforts on the Atlantic coast of North America, far from Shawnee territory. But as time went on, more and more Europeans came to the New World; 1.5 million, mostly Scotch-Irish and German, had arrived by 1760. The East Coast had grown so crowded that both newcomers and longtime colonists were moving west.

The British army, meanwhile, had already made its presence known in Shawnee territory—much to the chagrin of the French, who wanted the frontier to themselves. When the British built a fort in western Pennsylvania in 1754, the French promptly took it over. A garrison of Virginians, led by the youthful George Washington, marched in to retake it, only to find that the French had recruited the Shawnee, along with the Delaware and Seneca, to fight alongside them. Washington and his garrison went down in defeat, marking the beginning of what is now known in America as the French and Indian War.

Called the Seven Years' War in Europe, it was a seven-year struggle between the British and French for control of the American frontier. While the English controlled the eastern seaboard, French properties stretched as far as the Mississippi River. France was threatening to hem in Britain at the Appalachian Mountains. A great prize of this war was control of the fur trade.

A Shawnee named Puckeshinwa, father of Tecumseh and Tenkswatawa, made a valuable contribution to French efforts in Pennsylvania, and participated in a rematch the following year that turned into a rout for the French. However, despite French victories within the frontier, England emerged victorious by war's end.

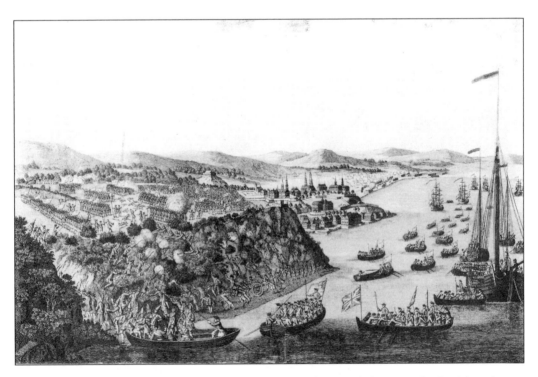

A battle of the French and Indian War, the seven-year struggle between the British and French for control over America. The Shawnee, Delaware, and Seneca tribes were recruited to fight for the French.

The War's Fallout

Despite their support of France, the Shawnee suffered relatively few casualties, particularly when compared to other tribes allied with the French. The Shawnee were then living in their home territory in Ohio, north of the Ohio River, between the Scioto and Miami Rivers, and controlling territory in what is now West Virginia, Kentucky, and Indiana.

But England's victory also meant that British settlers would begin to arrive unchecked in Shawnee territory. Over the years they would come by wagons and by river, despite the threat of Indian attack. Journalist Reuben Gold Thwaite, who traveled the Ohio River in the path of such settlers during the nineteenth century, displayed the prejudices of the time in his account of the troubles awaiting settlers who traveled by water. Thwaite wrote,

> Flatboats bearing traders, immigrants, and travelers were frequently waylaid by the savages who exhausted a fertile ingenuity in luring their victims [into an ambush]; and when not successful in this, would in narrow channels . . . subject the voyagers to a fierce fusillade of bullets, against which even stout plank barricades proved of small avail.[30]

To make matters even worse, the British Command in North America decided to treat the Shawnee and other tribes like conquered peoples. Goodwill presents, which had always been given to chiefs, abruptly ended and the supply of trade goods, upon which the Indians had come to depend, was restricted.

Pontiac's Rebellion

By the spring of 1763, the Indians had had enough. The Shawnee joined other tribes in the Midwest under the leadership of Pontiac, an Ottawa chief based out of Detroit. Known as Pontiac's Rebellion, the uprising caught the British by surprise. The Indian coalition took six of the nine British forts located west of the Appalachian mountain range. The Shawnee and their allies, who included the Delaware and Mingo, also hit the Pennsylvania frontier with a series of raids that killed six hundred white settlers.

But Pontiac's Rebellion collapsed after the Indians failed to take Fort Pitt in Pennsylvania, as well as forts in Niagara and Detroit. In August of that year, the Shawnee, Delaware, and Mingo were pushed out of Pennsylvania after a two-day battle near Fort Pitt. After Pontiac retreated to Indiana, the Shawnee signed a peace treaty with the British, who had been badly shaken up by the uprising. England issued a proclamation to its colonies prohibiting further settlement west of the Appalachian Mountains. But this order was ignored, causing no end of grief for both the Shawnee and the British. American colonists, including George Washington, had already staked land claims in the Ohio territory. Poorer frontiersmen had a simpler solution: Instead of purchasing land ahead of time, they simply moved west to settle and

A Gift of Smallpox?

During the conflict known as Pontiac's Rebellion, the Shawnee and other Indians were attacking British outposts in the Great Lakes region and the Midwest. In May 1763, they had targeted Fort Pitt, located in what is now Point State Park, Pittsburgh. In June, a smallpox outbreak forced the officer in charge to quarantine infected soldiers.

On June 24, two Delaware Indians, having failed in their mission to get the British to abandon the fort, asked for provisions for the trip home. They were given two blankets and a handkerchief that had been kept with the smallpox patients. Historians do not know who decided to give the infected blankets and handkerchief to the Indians. However, researchers have unearthed evidence that prior to the incident the British commander of Fort Pitt, Jeffrey Amherst, mentioned the idea in correspondence with a fellow officer in Philadelphia.

Just how many Indians ultimately died from this infected gift is unknown. But researchers say at least 120 Indians died within the year—forty apiece from the Shawnee, Mingo, and Delaware tribes.

The Shawnee confront British officers who gave them two blankets contaminated with smallpox.

farm, no matter what the British government told them.

Aftermath of a Rebellion

To combat what was already a relentless move westward, the Shawnee, Mingo, and Delaware banded together to face the Long Knives, their name for white frontiersmen. Meanwhile, the Iroquois, who by prior treaty still controlled Ohio territory, relinquished control to the British, who had been their allies since before the war.

The westward movement finally became official in 1774 when Lord Dunmore, colonial governor of Virginia, issued the first land grants in the Ohio River valley region. Virginians and Virginia surveying crews began a trek to the territory. The Shawnee, furious over the situation, resolved to defend their home. That same year, a band of Shawnee killed five out of six members of a Virginia surveying crew. Local whites retaliated by killing a group of Shawnee who had been on a peaceful mission to the British.

The territory was now aflame, and the Shawnee looked for assistance from their neighbors. They got help from the Mingo, whose chief, a once-peaceable man known as Logan, suffered a tragedy at the hands of the Europeans that same year. Logan had been away from his village along the Ohio when a drunken group of Virginians had come upon the village and murdered thirteen women and children, including Logan's entire family. Logan, a man well respected by the whites and Indians, went on a series of murderous raids against the American settlers. A white historian of the period wrote of Logan's revenge:

Logan now smothered down the promptings of his better nature. . . . Vengeance was his from the moment he heard the sad news of the killing of his relatives. Woe to the hapless victim upon the frontier, young, old, male or female, who should be startled by his war cry. [31]

A Decisive Battle

As Logan took his revenge, Dunmore saw a chance to take out the Ohio Indians for good. He sent three thousand troops into what became known as the Battle of Point Pleasant, named for a sandy spot on the Ohio and Great Kanawaha Rivers in West

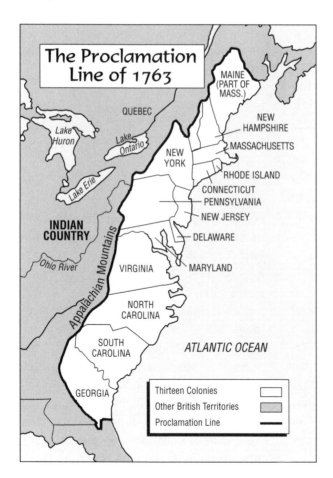

The Proclamation Line of 1763

MAINE (PART OF MASS.)
QUEBEC
NEW HAMPSHIRE
Lake Huron
Lake Ontario
MASSACHUSETTS
NEW YORK
Lake Erie
RHODE ISLAND
CONNECTICUT
PENNSYLVANIA
NEW JERSEY
INDIAN COUNTRY
DELAWARE
Ohio River
Appalachian Mountains
VIRGINIA
MARYLAND
NORTH CAROLINA
SOUTH CAROLINA
ATLANTIC OCEAN
GEORGIA

Thirteen Colonies
Other British Territories
Proclamation Line

Virginia. The Shawnee alliance, numbering seven hundred, met Dunmore's army there. Of the ensuing battle, Thwaite wrote:

> The combatants stood behind trees, in Indian fashion, and it is hard to say who displayed the better generalship, [the Shawnee chief] Cornstalk or Lewis [the British general]. When the pall of night covered this hideous contest, the whites had lost one-fifth of their number while the savages had sustained but half as many casualties. Cornstalk's followers had had enough, however, and withdrew before daylight.[32]

The Shawnee and their allies, including Logan, had acquitted themselves well. However, being that they were so vastly outnumbered, Chief Cornstalk decided to negotiate a peace settlement. Cornstalk, always an eloquent speaker, explained, "The Long Knives are upon us. . . . Shall We turn and fight them? Shall we kill our squaws and children and then fight until we are killed ourselves? . . . Since you are not inclined to fight I will go make peace."[33]

Cornstalk signed the Treaty of Camp Charlotte in November 1774. This agreement ceded all Shawnee claims to Kentucky. The tribe turned westward until their principal settlement was placed not along the Ohio, but the Little Miami River. And in time, their greatest trouble would not come from the British, but from a new American Republic.

The Shawnee and a Revolution

The American Revolution opened up a new chapter in relations between the Shawnee and England. It was settlers in North America, not the British government, who posed a threat to the Shawnee way of life. The British, at war with their colony, now encouraged Shawnee attacks on settlers, offering warriors a bounty on American prisoners and scalps. Yet the tribe was not officially at war with the Americans; Cornstalk, still a peacemaker, hoped to defuse the situation. In November 1777, he, his son, and another Shawnee went to Virginia to discuss the situation with American authorities. Officials promptly put them in prison, intending to hold them as hostages.

However, a mob broke into the room where the Shawnee were being kept and murdered them, beating and mutilating their bodies. Virginian Patrick Henry, who had replaced Dunmore as Virginia's governor, was distressed by the killings and immediately sued for peace. But he was too late: The tribe had already declared war against the colonists and formed an alliance with Britain.

Chief Blackfish, Cornstalk's replacement, led a series of raids in Kentucky and western Pennsylvania. In 1778, the Shawnee mounted a raid on Fort Randolph in Pennsylvania that was ultimately unsuccessful because the fort was so well fortified and because the American commander refused to let his men go out to fight. In 1779, John Bow-

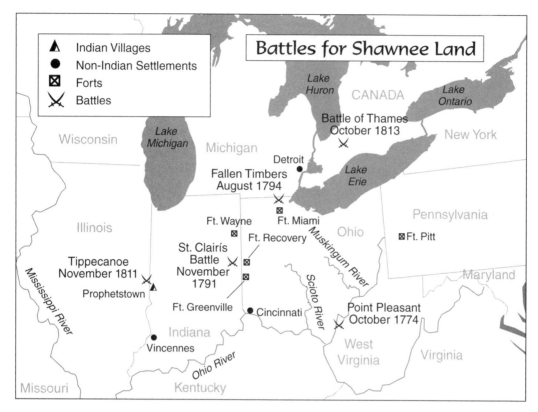

Battles for Shawnee Land

Legend:
- ▲ Indian Villages
- ● Non-Indian Settlements
- ⊠ Forts
- ✕ Battles

man and three hundred volunteers mounted their own raid against the Shawnee, crossing the Ohio River and burning the Indian village of Old Chillicothe. Blackfish was killed, and the Shawnee moved again, leaving their villages along the Scioto River.

The Shawnee Nation Divides

During the cycle of raids and reprisals that had begun before the Revolutionary War, a serious split in the Shawnee nation occurred. In March 1779, a Thawegila chief, speaking before a Shawnee council, made a very dramatic gesture, tomahawking a wampum belt in two. This act symbolized what many

Shawnee were feeling at the time. Unhappy with the military action of their leadership, many felt that the Americans, with their large numbers of men and weapons, would heap disaster upon the tribe. Thus, three of the five Shawnee clans decided they would rather leave than fight.

To implement this decision, the Thawegila, Piqua, and Kispoko clans, approximately four thousand people, or more than half the tribe, left Shawnee territory for southeastern Missouri. But the Chillicothe and Mekoce decided to stay, fight, and die rather than give up. They continued to fight, albeit in reduced numbers, alongside the British.

By this point, England was planning a three-pronged offensive to capture the Mississippi and Ohio River valleys. British captain Henry Bird left British headquarters in Detroit in April of 1779, marching southward with twelve hundred warriors, including Shawnee. This joint force burned many American settlements, killing residents along the way. When American general George Rogers Clark took his revenge, he did so against Shawnee villages along the Mad River. During this march he took just seven Shawnee prisoners; all other villagers were killed.

Yet just a few years after this massacre, the Treaty of Paris would be signed and the Revolutionary War would end. The

Daniel Boone Among the Shawnee

The life of legendary American frontiersman Daniel Boone often intertwined with the Shawnee during his time in the western frontier. In 1773, while leading a hunting expedition to the Kentucky territory, Boone lost his oldest son James in a skirmish with Shawnee braves. In spite of this loss, Boone moved the rest of his family into Indian territory, founding one of the first American settlements, Boonesborough, in Kentucky. But the Shawnee and Boone were not finished with one another. In 1777, Boone enacted a dramatic rescue of daughter Jemima and her companions, who had been kidnapped by a Shawnee hunting party. The following year Boone would be captured by the tribe. Chief Blackfish refused to turn him over to the British and adopted him as his own son. Although Boone later said he came to feel great affection for his Shawnee parents and siblings, he also had strong ties to the community that bore his name. Thus he escaped from his Shawnee family in June, in time to warn Boonesborough of an impending attack. The attack came in September, and while his warriors lay siege to Boonesborough for nine days, Blackfish stood outside the walls and berated Boone's ingratitude and his betrayal of his adopted father.

Like many frontiersmen, Boone always respected his Native American enemies. Boone would be on hand the night a group of Kentuckians captured Blue Jacket, who had been on a raid in Kentucky territory. The historical record suggests that Boone personally arranged for Blue Jacket to be imprisoned without guards and restrained lightly enough that the young Shawnee was able to escape unharmed.

Shawnee that remained began a new era at odds with the American government.

Some Unsatisfactory Treaties

The Treaty of Paris called for Britain to cede the Ohio valley lands to the United States. However, the agreement said nothing about, and did not include, the Indians who lived there. Soon the American government, needing monies to pay off the debts it had incurred during the war, decided to sell the Ohio property to settlers. Yet it needed the cooperation of the tribes who lived there. Since the Ohio tribes, including the Shawnee, were still considered allies of Great Britain, America had to negotiate with each tribe individually.

The Shawnee and their allies signed what would be known as the Greater Miami Treaty in 1785. The treaty put the boundaries for Indian territory at the Cuyahoga, Tuscarawas, and Muskingum Rivers. Both sides ended up dissatisfied with this arrangement: White settlers wanted the entire Ohio valley, while the Native Americans wanted their boundary to reach farther south, at the Ohio River instead of the Muskingum.

In November 1786, the Shawnee alliance sent a demand to Congress in Philadelphia that the boundary be extended to the Ohio River. They decided that if an answer was not received by spring, they would resume their attacks against settlers. July arrived, and still the Indians did not have their answer; according to historical accounts, the message of the alliance had still not reached Philadelphia. Thus, Shawnee warriors, joined by the Mingo and Chickamauga, raided Kentucky settlements throughout the spring and summer. An American colonel, Benjamin Logan, retaliated by attacking and burning Shawnee villages.

In 1789, the Shawnee alliance and America signed another treaty which again established the Muskingum as a boundary river. But this latest agreement changed nothing: Settlers felt entitled to all of the Ohio territory, yet the tribes still wanted their boundary at the Ohio. By summertime, the Shawnee and Miami reached a consensus among themselves: They would go to war. And although Britain had conceded defeat to the United States, they kept enough of a presence in the western territory that the tribes could still pledge their help and support.

The Shawnee Return to War

Shawnee chief Blue Jacket and Miami chief Little Turtle led thousands of warriors from the Shawnee, Miami, and other tribes in a string of startling victories. In 1791, they would hand American leader Arthur St. Clair a crushing defeat in western Ohio. President George Washington, dismayed by the Indians' successes, sent in a new commander, "Mad" Anthony Wayne. Wayne established himself at Fort Greeneville, eighty miles north of Cincinnati, in the spring of 1794. In July, he left Greeneville to build more forts to support his advance

"Mad" Anthony Wayne

The victor at Fallen Timbers is probably known best for his unusual nickname—given, it is said, because he had such a hot temper. But Wayne also served in the Revolutionary War and counted among his friends and acquaintances America's founding fathers. Born in Pennsylvania, Wayne served for a time as a surveyor for Benjamin Franklin in Nova Scotia. In 1775, he was one of four men chosen to head up a battalion in the Continental Army. His regiment served in the campaign against Quebec, and Wayne stayed in the fray despite a serious leg wound.

Wayne, called the "chief who never sleeps" by the Native Americans, would be tapped by President George Washington to lead the American forces against the Shawnee and Miami alliance following the disastrous defeat of Arthur St. Clair. The American victory at Fallen Timbers was also a fatal blow to the British, who still maintained frontier forts, including Fort Miami, near Fallen Timbers. Wayne's victory is credited with helping to end British power in the West.

Wayne died of gout in 1796 at the age of fifty-one. He was buried in Erie, Pennsylvania, but thirteen years later his son Isaac decided to move the body to the family burial plot in Radnor. His son had traveled to Erie in a one-horse carriage to claim the body. Since the carriage was so small, Isaac Wayne's companion dissected the body and boiled its parts to render the flesh from the bones. The flesh was reburied in the Erie grave, and Wayne's skeleton was taken back to Radnor. Legend has it that some bones fell out of the carriage during the trip home, and that every New Year's morning, Wayne's ghost rides between Radnor and Erie, on present-day Route 322, looking for his lost bones.

A portrait of Anthony Wayne, whose ghost is sometimes seen roaming the Pennsylvania countryside.

against the Indians. Some alliance leaders, such as Little Turtle, argued for caution, but the rank and file, as well as Blue Jacket himself, were still determined to fight, despite that they had already lost many warriors because there was not enough food to feed them. Also, the Kickapoo had been forced to withdraw support because so many of their women and children had been taken hostage by the Americans.

But Blue Jacket pressed on. In August of 1794, he brought seven hundred warriors to a conflict known as the Battle of Fallen Timbers, named for the number of trees in the area that had been uprooted by a tornado. Wayne's army, which outnumbered Blue Jacket's men, attacked at mid-morning. Following the Indians' retreat, Wayne spent three days destroying their crops and villages.

Surrender

The Shawnee and their allies were forced to make a final surrender in 1795. Blue Jacket and his fellow chiefs signed the treaty at

The Shawnee suffered a crushing defeat at the Battle of Fallen Timbers (pictured).

Greeneville, Ohio, which ceded all Ohio lands, save the northwest corner. But Tecumseh, then a rising young warrior, did not. Tecumseh, of course, made a remarkable, though unsuccessful, last stand against the whites. Tecumseh's death in 1813 would end any hopes of the Shawnee regaining their lands. Less than twenty years after his death, the last remaining Ohio Shawnee were forced westward, into strange territory, which even then would not be their own.

Chapter 5

Tecumseh, the Prophet, and Exile in the West

Tecumseh, the most famous Shawnee of all, wanted his people to regain control of their lands and destiny, and hoped to do so by creating an alliance of Indian nations strong enough to stand up to the U.S. government. This dream collapsed, however, and Tecumseh allied with the British during the War of 1812, reasoning that a British victory could return the Shawnee to their homeland. When Tecumseh was killed in 1813, the remaining Ohio chief, Black Hoof, tried to keep the whites at bay. But the Indian Removal Act of the 1830s forced the Shawnee to move west. They were eventually reunited with the Shawnee who had preceded them, though tensions remained. The tribe moved several times during these years; the government would assign them land only to order them off when it was targeted for other purposes. The Shawnee nation eventually fragmented a second time into three groups (which still exist today): the Loyal or Cherokee Shawnee, now called the Shawnee Tribe, the Absentee Shawnee, and the Eastern Shawnee.

The tribe's fate was a far cry from what Tecumseh had envisioned: The Shawnee regained peace and power.

Two Chiefs, Two Strategies

Two prominent Shawnee emerged after the Greeneville treaty: Tecumseh, a Thawegila who had remained in Ohio, and Black Hoof, a Mekoce. The two warrior heroes had different ideas on how to deal with whites. Black Hoof preferred to keep the peace, though he was hardly an appeaser. During a visit to Washington, D.C., in 1802, he startled Secretary of War Henry Dearborn by asking for a deed to Shawnee lands in Ohio. His request was denied.

Black Hoof struggled to protect his people during some very difficult times. Rhodes, who met with Black Hoof in Ohio in 1817, wrote, "From every appearance he was greatly concerned for the welfare of his people he looked as solid and grave as I ever saw a minister, which made serious impressions on my mind." [34]

Tecumseh had a much different vision for his people. He wanted to unite Native Americans politically, form a nation to occupy what was left of Indian territory, and stop the advancement of whites. He spent much of his time traveling from tribe to tribe, speaking of unity and the evil that the whites brought upon the Indians. He said,

> Shall we calmly wait until they become so numerous that we will no longer be able to resist oppression? Will we wait to be destroyed in our turn, without making an effort worthy of our race? . . . Never! Never! Then let us [with] units of action destroy them all.[35]

Tecumseh did not advocate war for war's sake. His mission was to convince the whites that if they did not mend their ways, a terrible war—with all the Indian nations united—would occur. He did not want to provoke the Americans into making preemptive strikes. Nor did he want his people to make preemptive strikes of their own. He preferred, rather, that the Native Americans put aside their differences, unite as a federation, and be ready to fight if necessary.

Not all Shawnee agreed with Tecumseh. Historians have contended that most of the remaining Ohio Shawnee preferred Black Hoof's strategy. However, thirteen years after the Greeneville treaty, Tecumseh enjoyed broad support, not only among the Shawnee, but among other

Mekoce chief Black Hoof aimed to keep the peace between Indians and white settlers.

Tecumseh, the Man

The most famous Shawnee chief was probably born in 1768—no one knows exactly—in the Ohio River valley region. He was the fourth child of Methoastaske and the Shawnee warrior Puckeshinwa. Tecumseh's name, also spelled Tekamthi, has been translated into English as Celestial Panther, Shooting Star, Crouching Panther, and Man Who Waits. His brother, Lalawethika, was one of a set of triplets born to the couple, such an unusual occurrence for the Shawnee that Lalawethika was thought to be destined for great things. Tecumseh, however, would rise to prominence first.

As an adult, Tecumseh apparently married twice. He fathered his son Pachetha with first wife Mamete, who is thought to have died while Pachetha was still a child. Tecumseh's second marriage may have lasted about five years; biographers say he was so involved in tribal affairs that a personal life became impossible. Tecumseh had been part of the important victory over Arthur St. Clair in 1791. After Fallen Timbers, the Shawnee chief became a vocal opponent of further white expansion. He resisted signing the Greeneville treaty, and, with the help of his brother, who was by then the main Shawnee spiritual leader, set about forming a confederacy among Native Americans west of the Appalachian Mountains and east of the Mississippi River.

Tecumseh had frequent contact with white leaders because of his high-profile position. They were so impressed with his intelligence, compassion, and eloquence that, in accordance with the prejudice of the day, rumors surfaced he had white blood. Tecumseh fascinated people even after his death, as white journalists and historians compared his skills to those of European military leaders and generals. Books about Tecumseh continue to be written today, and his ideas and life have raised public awareness of his people and their plight.

Tecumseh resisted white expansion and formed a confederacy among Native Americans.

Indiana governor William Henry Harrison was an enemy of the Shawnee.

A Brother and a Prophet

Tenkswatawa, also known as the Shawnee Prophet, added a spiritual component to Tecumseh's political plans. While Tecumseh preached Indian solidarity, Tenkswatawa advocated a return to a traditional way of life, free of white influence. Both men inspired great loyalty among their followers, which were becoming numerous by the early 1800s.

Harrison became particularly alarmed when the brothers moved their followers to the banks of the Wabash River in Indiana, his territory. Harrison sent spies to this community, known as Prophetstown, in 1809. He learned that more than three thousand warrior-supporters from various tribes had relocated there in response to Tecumseh's call for a confederacy.

Indians in the region, and from the British, who promised to help him fight against Americans. Most of Tecumseh's non-Shawnee recruits came from Ohio, Kentucky, and Indiana—territory whites had been trying to settle since before the French and Indian War.

Tecumseh's ideas had been successful enough that white leaders, including Indiana governor William Henry Harrison, were watching him—and his brother Tenkswatawa—closely.

That same year, Harrison signed treaties with the Delaware, Miami, Kaskaskia, and Potawatomi at Fort Wayne and Vincennes. The agreements, which ceded 3 million acres of southern Indiana and Illinois, enraged Tecumseh. Harrison and the chief held a meeting at Vincennes in August, and the words between them were harsh. They met again three years later, in 1811, to no avail. After that meeting, Tecumseh traveled south to try to gain support for his confederacy plans from the Chickasaw, Choctaw, Creek, and Cherokee. He gave his brother specific instructions that, during his absence, the Prophetstown warriors should avoid confronting the Americans.

But one thousand of Harrison's men were already bound for Prophetstown. They regarded Tecumseh's absence as a prime opportunity.

A Battle at Tippecanoe

Harrison and his men arrived in the fall of 1811, camping across Tippecanoe Creek. Tecumseh biographer Gilbert speculated what could have gone through Tenkswatawa's mind at that point. Gilbert wrote,

He had grown up awkward and disfigured, incompetent at traditional manly pursuits. Then miraculously, he had emerged as a messenger and confidant of the gods. But after only a few years of prominence, he had returned to a position where he received and was expected to obey the orders of Tecumseh, the brilliant older brother in whose long shadow he spent most of his life.[36]

For reasons unknown, Tenkswatawa ignored his brother's orders and incited the warriors to stand and fight. He had had a vision, he told them. The Great Spirit would cover the field with a magic fog whereby the warriors' vision would be enhanced, the whites' blinded.

A fierce battle followed in which 50 Americans died and 130 were wounded. Indian casualties were 40 dead, and more wounded. Two hours into the battle the Indians retreated. Tenkswatawa remained on a small knoll nearby asking for the Great Spirit's assistance. Most of the warriors left Prophetstown, and some spread the story that the Shawnee was a coward, and a false prophet.

Tenkswatawa and his remaining followers retreated about ten miles south as Harrison and his men burned Prophetstown. Tecumseh returned to Indiana in January of 1812, but the damage was done: Tecumseh's confederation plans were in shambles, and the War of 1812 was just months away.

The Death of Tecumseh

The War of 1812 arose because of quarrels between America and Great Britain over what Americans saw as British interference with U.S. trade and over England's encouragement of rebellious Indian tribes on the American frontier. Still hoping for Indian independence, Tecumseh allied himself with Great Britain since England had supported the Shawnee in the past. He particularly valued the support of a British official, Major General Isaac Brock, who favored the idea of a neutral Indian nation and welcomed Tecumseh's help. He and Tecumseh had fought together in Detroit and in Ohio. But Brock's death early in the war forced Tecumseh to deal with British generals much less sympathetic to the Indians' cause. However, Tecumseh and Tenkswatawa, who remained with his brother, recruited two thousand warriors to the British cause.

On October 5, 1813, Tecumseh, his warriors, and British soldiers fought

American troops on the banks of the Thames River in Canada. Harrison, Tecumseh's old enemy, led the American army. His troops included a regiment of mounted Kentucky riflemen, so well trained they could charge right into a line of firing soldiers. The Kentucky cavalry attacked around 2:30 P.M., sweeping through the lines and taking prisoners.

Tecumseh and his warriors held their ground well, protected by the surrounding underbrush. But after much intense fighting word spread that Tecumseh had fallen. His forces surrendered and what happened next remains controversial nearly two hundred years later. The Kentuckians found a body on the battlefield they believed to be Tecumseh's. But Harrison, who knew the

William Henry Harrison leads his troops in the battle at Tippecanoe. The aftermath of this battle resulted in the failure of Tecumseh's confederation plans.

Tecumseh is killed during the Battle of the Thames. The chief's final resting place remains unknown to this day.

chief, could not confirm the identification. An Indian interpreter later claimed that Tecumseh's body had been carried off the field and that the Americans had found the body of his aide, a Potawatomi chief. If Tecumseh's body was indeed recovered and buried, his grave remains a secret to this day.

His death had far-reaching consequences for his people. Just nineteen years later, like other eastern tribes, the Shawnee would be forced, by way of threats and coercion, to move west.

The Absentee Shawnee

Black Hoof remained leader of the Ohio Shawnee after Tecumseh's death. Most respected his decision to stay in their home territory. Some, however, decided to leave Ohio immediately. These Shawnee went west to Missouri to join the divisions of Shawnee who had arrived in the eighteenth century. Having not lived together in years, tensions simmered between the Ohio and Missouri Shawnee. By 1822, a group of Missouri Shawnee had left the territory for Texas, then part of Mexico.

In Texas they joined an Indian alliance led by the Cherokee. The Mexican government had promised this alliance a parcel of land in return for their allegiance to Mexico. When the Mexicans reneged, the Indians switched their support to the Texas Independence movement.

After Texas won its independence from Mexico in 1830, the Indians enjoyed a brief period of good treatment from Texas's first governor, Sam Houston. But Houston's successor, Mirabeau Lamar, drove the Indians out of Texas in 1839. The former Missouri Shawnee retreated to a site in Oklahoma along the Canadian River. This group formed the nucleus of what became known as the Absentee Shawnee, named such because they were "absent" from treaty negotiations that gave the Shawnee land in Kansas—land that the Absentees had never seen. A group of Ohio Shawnee *had* arrived in Kansas during the 1820s, led by none other than Tenkswatawa.

The Prophet's Return

Tenkswatawa had remained in Canada after the war, unwilling to live in Ohio under the governance of Black Hoof, his late brother's rival. But he chafed under the supervision of the British, and in 1824, accepted Ohio governor Lewis Cass's invitation to return home. Tenkswatawa promised the governor he would try to convince the remaining Ohio Shawnee to cross the Mississippi, thus releasing their land to settlers.

The Shawnee who had remained in Missouri, known as the Black Bob Band, had already been forcibly removed after Missouri became a state. The government had decreed that all Shawnee Missouri lands were federal property. And the Black Bob Shawnee were sent to a twenty-five hundred square-mile parcel in Kansas. Tenkswatawa led a combined group of Shawnee and Mingo to Kansas in 1828, hoping that the tribe would look to him for leadership once again. But it was not to be, for while his fellow Shawnee did not disrespect him, they had turned their attention to other leaders. As Sugden wrote,

> [The Prophet] became lonely, "silent and melancholy," dwelling in the past, and regaling occasional visitors with stories about Tecumseh. His brother, he said, had been a great general, and were it not for his death he would have built a mighty confederacy from the Great Lakes to Mexico. [37]

Absentees in the Civil War

In his later years the Shawnee Prophet would become somewhat of a Kansas tourist attraction, with scores of frontier artists showing up at his home, clamoring to sketch him. But the Shawnee, particularly the Absentees, had serious issues to worry about. The American Civil War was brewing, and conflicts between abolitionists and the pro-slavery faction had reached Oklahoma territory. The Shawnee gave their support to the Union and many of their men fought in the federal army. But their neighbors, the Creek, supported the Confederacy. The Creek attacked the Shawnee so often over this issue

A Family Tradition

The youngest of Tecumseh's grandchildren, Wapameepto, which means "Gives Light as He Walks" in Shawnee, inherited his famous grandfather's instincts for rebellion. Wapameepto's father was Pachetha, who lived for a number of years with his uncle Tenkswatawa in Kansas before moving to a settlement along the Sabine River in Texas. There he married and fathered six children, the youngest of whom was Wapameepto.

Called Big Jim by the white community, Wapameepto was one of the most conservative Shawnee of his generation. He refused to farm with a horse and plow, like the whites. He told federal Indian agents that the earth was his mother, and to plow it was to cut up and scar the maternal planet. Wapameepto became ringleader for a band of Shawnee who hunted, foraged, and farmed the traditional way.

A member of the Absentee Shawnee, Wapameepto became increasingly bitter over their treatment by the U.S. government. A group of white speculators, seeing their chance to snap up Absentee lands, tried to convince the tribe to abandon Oklahoma for northern Mexico. There, the speculators said, they would be free to live as they wished. Most of the Absentees stayed put, but Wapameepto, his family, and other like-minded Shawnee decided to move. Wapameepto led the small group, which included women and children, but their bid for freedom ended in tragedy when they unknowingly trekked into a territory rife with the smallpox virus. All but two members of the group died of that deadly disease, including Wapameepto.

The grandson of Tecumseh, Wapameepto practiced traditional Shawnee ways.

that some of the Absentees even left their lands in Oklahoma for the relative safety of the Kansas Shawnee community.

After the war ended, however, the land situation in Oklahoma Indian territory grew even more crowded—and became worse once the Kansas Shawnee were forced to move there. Those few Absentees still living in Kansas rejoined their fellow tribesmen on their Oklahoma lands and some members of the Black Bob band became Absentees. The remaining Black Bob members joined up with two other groups of Shawnee, later known as the Loyal or Cherokee Shawnee, and the Eastern Shawnee. They also moved to Oklahoma after an enforced relocation to the West prompted by the Indian Removal Act.

Early Results of the Indian Removal Act

Congress passed the Indian Removal Act in 1830 with the enthusiastic support of President Andrew Jackson, a longtime Indian foe. Called Sharp Knife by his Native American enemies, Jackson had made it his business to push Indians out of territory east of the Mississippi during the War of 1812. The Indian Removal Act had tragic consequences for the Indians, particularly the Cherokee, whose forced march westward became known as the Trail of Tears.

The elderly Black Hoof, after working for years to keep peace with the Americans, resisted all efforts to force him and his people out of Ohio. He and his people remained in their settlements at Wapakoneta and Hog Creek, trying hard to live within the confines the government had given them. The tribe was under pressure in more ways than one: Like other tribes, they were being asked to adopt white ways, even in so far as the way they grew their food. Rhodes described the experience of Black Hoof's people in growing wheat, not a traditional Shawnee crop. The Indians had not harvested wheat before and welcomed Rhodes's help. Rhodes wrote,

> Today I was at a reaping at the great chief's Black Hoof; there was upwards of 20 Indians. . . . I showed them how to reap which they were anxious to know, also how to make bands and bind a sheaf, likewise how to put up a shock, [a task in] which there was great room for amendment. . . . I suppose the whole company had reaped half of an acre but had not shocked much of it. [38]

After Black Hoof's death, the last of his people, about six hundred of them, were sent from Ohio to Kansas, to a site along the Kaw River, in 1832. The federal government wanted to send them west by steamboat, but the Indians refused; they preferred horseback. One of the women explained her feelings to the authorities. She said,

> We will not go by steamboats, nor will we go in wagons, but we will go on horseback. It is the most agreeable manner for us, and if we are not allowed to go so, we can and will remain here and die and be buried with our relatives; it will be but a short

A Shawnee Mission in Kansas

Methodist missionary Thomas Johnson achieved a goal in 1839 when a Shawnee mission school site was chosen in Johnson County, Kansas, along a branch of the Santa Fe Trail near Kansas City. Though built for the Shawnee, with whom Johnson had long been involved, the school accepted students from other area tribes, including the Delaware, Ottawa, Chippewa, and Cherokee. In its heyday the mission school served nearly two hundred students on a two-thousand-plus-acre site, with twelve buildings.

Students worked for their keep at the school: Boys did farm chores and girls sewed and cooked. In addition to more traditional subjects, girls learned spinning and weaving while boys worked in the smokehouse, springhouse, and blacksmith and wagon shops. A visitor to the school in 1855 remarked that mission students differed little from those in other Kansas schools. The new territorial governor—Kansas had become a U.S. territory a year earlier—opened his offices at the mission, and the territorial legislature met on its grounds.

Johnson turned the school over to his oldest son, Alexander, in 1858. The mission closed four years later, and on January 2, 1865, Johnson was murdered in his home by Southern sympathizers angered that Johnson, a proslavery man for years, had sworn an oath of allegiance to the Union. He was buried in the mission's cemetery along with several members of his family. Although deeded to the Johnson family, the mission property was acquired by the state of Kansas as a historical site in 1927.

time before we leave this world anyway, and let us avert from our heads as much necessary pain and sorrow as possible.[39]

They were allowed to keep their horses, but this would be one of the last favors ever given to them. The government had promised provisions and tools in their new home, but these would not be forthcoming. The houses promised to them in Kansas had not been built, and no crosscut saws, grindstones, or rifles—also part of the agreement—ever arrived. Quaker missionaries sympathetic to the tribe did pitch in to help that winter, and years later, in an account of their mission penned by a Kansas author, damned the government's treatment of the Shawnee. "It is a blot on the page of history how the government agents wronged this helpless people,"[40] writes author Flora Kittle, in her book *The Shawnee Indians in Kansas.*

Forced to Move Again

Authorities did build a sawmill on Shawnee land in 1833, so as to provide wood for the tribe's cabins, but deducted money for its construction from a payment the tribe had been slated to receive upon moving to Kansas. Then, in 1854, the tribe was forced to move again. Plans were underway to open Kansas and Nebraska to white settlement and once again the former Ohio Shawnee were in the way of white expansion. The treaty they were forced to sign deeded their 1.6 million Kansas acres to the federal government for less than one dollar an acre.

The Ohio Shawnee were pushed onto Absentee lands in Kansas. They, too, supported the Union in the Civil War, so tensions were high in Kansas, even on Shawnee lands. The Methodist mission school which ministered to the Shawnee and other Indians would be accused of harboring slaves, and its founder, a white missionary who was pro-Union, murdered. Nonetheless, the former followers of Black Hoof proved valuable supporters of the Union army, and many of their men served honorably for the North.

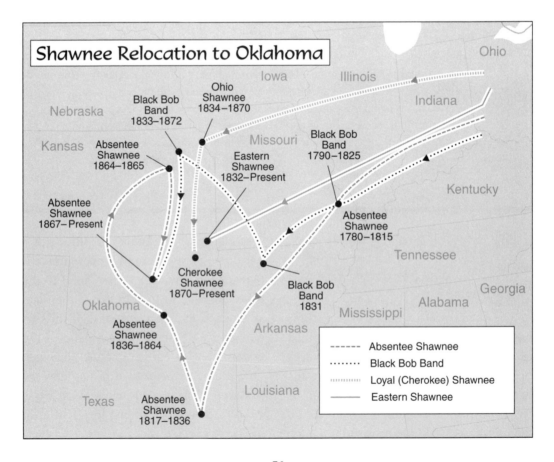

Shawnee Relocation to Oklahoma

Ohio

Iowa Illinois

Ohio Shawnee 1834–1870

Black Bob Band 1833–1872

Nebraska

Indiana

Kansas Absentee Shawnee 1864–1865

Missouri

Black Bob Band 1790–1825

Eastern Shawnee 1832–Present

Kentucky

Absentee Shawnee 1867–Present

Absentee Shawnee 1780–1815

Tennessee

Cherokee Shawnee 1870–Present

Black Bob Band 1831

Georgia

Oklahoma

Alabama

Mississippi

Absentee Shawnee 1836–1864

Arkansas

- - - - - Absentee Shawnee
········ Black Bob Band
▩▩▩▩▩ Loyal (Cherokee) Shawnee
——— Eastern Shawnee

Louisiana

Texas Absentee Shawnee 1817–1836

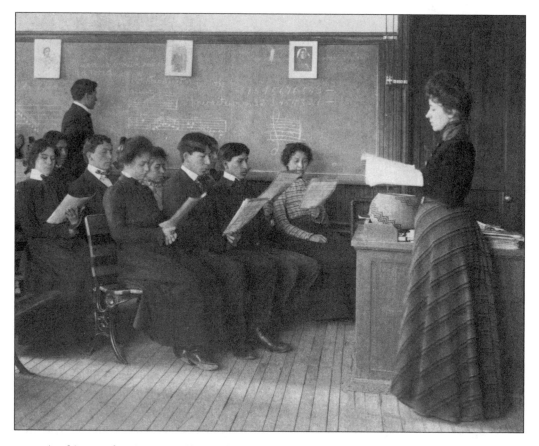

A white teacher instructs Native American students. For years the Shawnee resisted assimilation.

In 1869, after the Absentees had gone to Oklahoma, the government resettled the former Ohio Shawnee in Cherokee territory in Oklahoma. This decision was apparently to reward them for their loyal service during the war—hence, the term "Loyal" Shawnee. However, the government had a dual purpose: policymakers wished to punish the pro-Confederacy Cherokee by placing Shawnees in their territory. The Absentees, who had been equally loyal to the Union, received no

such "reward." The move also allowed the government to handle Shawnee affairs under the auspices of the Cherokee nation.

Because they lived in Cherokee territory, Loyal Shawnee were also called the Cherokee Shawnee by white outsiders. The Loyal Shawnee, re-recognized as a nation separate from the Cherokee in 2000, are now called the Shawnee Tribe. They have lived in Oklahoma since the post–Civil War era but they, like the Absentees, were preceded in that state by a mixed band of Seneca and Shawnee who left Ohio in 1831.

Eastern Shawnee

This third Shawnee group, now known as the Eastern Shawnee, lived with a band of friendly Seneca in the area of Lewiston, Ohio. Like the Black Hoof Shawnee, they fiercely resisted a move westward. But after passage of the Indian Removal Act, pressure became too great and the Seneca-Shawnee band was sent directly to northeastern Oklahoma. The Shawnee separated from the Seneca thirty-five years later to form the nucleus of the Eastern Shawnee. The Seneca in turn joined with other Seneca from the Sandusky, Ohio, area to form the Seneca-Cayuga Tribe of Oklahoma.

Though the three factions of Shawnee arrived in Oklahoma at different times and in different ways, all went on to fiercely resist the pressure to adapt to white culture. The Shawnee in all three groups refused to learn English, send their children to white schools, or convert to Christianity. They continued to hunt and farm in the way they always had, even as white towns and settlements built up around them. Their stubbornness caught notice from the world around them. As Protestant minister Josh Spencer noted, "The Shawnees cling to their old customs, seemingly more reluctant to abandon their ancient rites than any other civilized tribes." [41]

Assimilation did occur over time, particularly since the Shawnee, despite the existence of tribal lands, do not live on reservations. Hence, tribal members live in white communities and must work at white jobs and professions in order to survive in American society. Their children attend white schools and most have not grown up hearing the Shawnee language. Yet, the Shawnee people continue to practice their culture, and in some cases, their native tongue, even as the tribe pursues economic independence that will help it survive and prosper in a twenty-first-century white world.

Chapter 6

A Nation Continues

White outsiders have called the Shawnee one of the best-housed and one of the more financially well-off Indian tribes in America. This may well be true, but outside help has counted for very little. The hard work of Shawnee leaders and ordinary tribal members has been mainly responsible for the successes their people enjoy.

Tribal officials have noted that since the 1960s, federal Indian policy has focused on self-determination, though federal funding to help tribes achieve this goal has been scanty. Like other tribes, the Eastern Shawnee and the Absentee Shawnee have used revenue from casino establishments built on tribal lands to develop social service programs and educational support for tribal members. As of 2002, the Shawnee Tribe, formerly the Loyal Shawnee, newly emerged from the Cherokee nation, was just beginning to develop a set of economic plans for the tribe and its members.

While the Shawnee have learned how to live and work in the white world, what the tribe wishes most is to remain Shawnee.

Federal Indian Policies

The Shawnee have struggled to remain a culturally viable tribe through decades of unhelpful and inconsistent federal policies. By the end of the nineteenth century, federal Indian policy was openly suppressive: U.S. authorities would do what they could, for the good of the country and for, it was thought, the good of the Indians themselves, to eliminate tribal organizations and landholdings, and to do away with Indian customs, spiritual beliefs, and traditions. Schools like the boarding school run by the Methodists for the Shawnee and other Indians outside Kansas City were encouraged, as they would assimilate young Indian children and "prepare" them for white society.

Yet, by the 1920s, some whites were questioning the bureaucratic umbrella that had been erected over America's Indian nations. In 1934, President

A Serpentine Mound

The Fort Ancient culture, the prehistoric tribe that historians believe were forerunners to the Shawnee, can be studied closely thanks to the artifacts and settlements they left behind. One of the most famous is the Great Serpent Mound in Peebles, Ohio, located in Adams County along State Road 73.

The mound is one of the more mysterious artifacts that the Fort Ancients, who flourished in northern Kentucky and southern Ohio until 1650, left behind. The mound resembles a giant snake uncoiling and is nearly a quarter of a mile long. The Great Serpent can be perceived and followed on the ground but is best appreciated from the air. It averages three feet in height along its entire length and overlooks the valley of Brush Creek. It is surrounded by burial mounds and artifacts of an even earlier people: the Adena, who lived in Ohio from 800 B.C. to A.D. 100.

Just what the mound signifies or represents, is debatable. But archaeologists believe that it had religious or spiritual significance to the people who built it. Oddly enough, despite the existence of the Great Serpent, the Fort Ancients were not the prodigious mound builders, like their predecessors, the Adena. The Fort Ancients made their settlements look like a fort: They built houses around an open plaza. They built small burial mounds early in their culture, but eventually came to bury their dead in a "cemetery area" within their territory, a cemetery that did not include burial mounds.

The Great Serpent Mound is believed to have been built by the Fort Ancients or the Adena.

Dressed in fashions of the day, a group of Shawnee poses for a photo. Throughout the nineteenth century, the Shawnee were pressured into assimilating into American society.

Franklin D. Roosevelt signed the Indian Reorganization Act, which reversed the country's longtime policy of assimilating the Indians and seizing their land at will. Day schools, instead of boarding schools, were encouraged for Indian students so that they could live with their families. In the U.S. Department of the Interior, officials were encouraged to hire Native Americans for jobs in the Bureau of Indian Affairs.

Despite this new, more enlightened outlook, some destructive practices continued. For example, boarding schools for Indian students continued to operate into the 1970s. And during the 1950s the notion of assimilating the Shawnee and other Native Americans regained favor among government officials. Congress established the Voluntary Relocation Program in 1952, which offered assistance to Native Americans who agreed to move from tribal lands and into urban areas. About a decade later, though, the government changed directions again, deciding that the best course of action for the Indians and the nation was a policy called self-determination. Under this policy, Indian tribes would eventually move toward self-government and toward developing their own economic resources.

This approach became increasingly difficult to implement as funds for federal housing and job training programs of the 1970s were cut by the Reagan administration during the 1980s. But during that same time, the government paved the way for American Indian tribes to pursue money-making ventures, namely gambling casinos, on tribal property.

Indian Gaming

In 1988, Congress passed the Indian Gaming Regulatory Act, which recognizes the right of tribes to establish gambling and gaming facilities in states that allow gambling. This act was passed after two tribes, the Seminole of Florida and the Cabazon band of Mission Indians of southern California, won lawsuits involving gaming on tribal lands. Supporters of Native Americans hoped that Indian-run casinos would help lift the low standard of living on the Indian reservations. As journalist Anne Merline

The Eastern Shawnee gaming hall, Bordertown Bingo, in West Seneca, Oklahoma. Indian tribes have the legal right to establish gambling and gaming facilities.

McCulloch described the situation in 1994, "It is widely known that Indians living on the reservations have the highest unemployment rate in the nation and the lowest life expectancy rate. Reservations are often compared to Third World Nations."[42]

Indian gaming has remained a controversial issue. Critics contend that the casinos and bingo halls have driven up crime and gambling addiction rates in the communities that host them. Supporters, however, point to the tribal jobs and cash generated by such ventures. For example, the Absentee and Eastern Shawnee, in addition to running successful gaming establishments, now run other businesses as well as social and educational programs for tribal members.

The Absentee casino, the Thunderbird, is located in Norman, Oklahoma, south of Oklahoma City, and features games, entertainment, and a restaurant. The Eastern Shawnee operate their gaming hall, Bordertown Bingo, in West Seneca, Oklahoma. Both groups chose to build their casinos near their respective tribal offices and headquarters.

Divisional Alignments Today

Each of the three Shawnee groups owns a complex of offices, land, and buildings, and members tend to live within their own divisional headquarters. Although over the years tribal members have intermarried with other Indians—as well as whites and blacks—Absentees, Easterns, and Loyals still invariably identify themselves as Shawnee.

The Absentee Shawnee, whose tribal rolls record two thousand members, include descendants of the Thawegila, Piqua, and Kispoko divisions of Shawnee who left the Ohio territory in the eighteenth century. Today's Absentees divide themselves into two groups: the Big Jim and White Turkey bands.

The Big Jim band settled into the area of Hog Creek and Little River in Oklahoma, east of Norman, when, in the late 1800s, the U.S. military forced them out of lands they had occupied on the Deep Fork River, also in Oklahoma. At first called the Big Jim settlement, the area was renamed Little Axe. The White Turkey band had stayed in Pottawatomie County, near the town of Shawnee, Oklahoma. Both groups, however, look to the Norman offices as their center of government.

The Eastern Shawnee headquarters, servicing eighteen hundred members, is located in West Seneca, Oklahoma. The traditional Chillicothe and Mekoce divisions can mostly be found among either the Easterns or the Shawnee Tribe of Oklahoma, the former Loyal Shawnee who in 2000 became known as the Shawnee Tribe.

Separate Status for Some

The former Loyal Shawnee have experienced the greatest number of changes in recent years, particularly in 2000, when they were granted separate status from the Cherokee. The Shawnee Tribe held their first annual meeting independent of the Cherokee on September 16, 2001, in

A Shawnee Buffalo Herd

Most Americans today think the buffalo, more properly known as the American bison, is a creature native to the Far West. But in the seventeenth and eighteenth centuries, small herds of buffalo ranged across Ohio and as far east as Georgia. Historians estimate that before the whites arrived, 30 to 70 million bison roamed America. Indian tribes such as the Shawnee hunted the buffalo, just as they did waterfowl, bear, and deer, and depended on its meat for sustenance and its fur for warmth. But by 1800, the buffalo was extinct east of the Mississippi River, the victim of overhunting by Europeans intent on protecting their livestock and farmlands.

Thirty years later, organized buffalo hunting for hides and meat had become widespread in the West. There were reports that up to 250 animals would be killed in one day. By 1900, less than a thousand bison remained in the American West.

A rescue and restoration program was begun in the twentieth century; today, most buffalo live in national parks and on private lands. In 1999, the Loyal or Cherokee Shawnee, now known as the Shawnee Tribe of Oklahoma, acquired a small buffalo herd of its own. The nineteen bison were acquired through the Inter-Tribal Bison Cooperative, which awarded the tribe a grant in 2002. The grant money will be used to purchase fencing, a storage barn, a tractor, supplemental feed, and veterinary services. The tribe hopes to eventually use the herd for tribal functions, and to serve buffalo meat in tribal elders' meal programs. The Shawnee Tribe of Oklahoma would eventually like to support a herd of one hundred animals.

White Oak, Oklahoma. The tribe has its office in Miami, Oklahoma, and a community building in White Oak. The Shawnee Tribe had thirteen hundred members on its tribal rolls in 2002. About six to seven thousand Cherokee Shawnee had yet to transfer from the Cherokee nation, the auspices of which their families had lived under for generations. This new Shawnee tribe faced a number of obstacles as they stepped out on their own, in part because while they have been given federal recognition, they received no federal funding.

To complicate matters, the government never transferred the tribe's legal authority to Oklahoma. Rather, this authority, which would allow the Shawnee Tribe of Oklahoma to operate business ventures, is still in Kansas, the state where the Loyals initially lived.

Tribal Plans for the Twenty-First Century

The Shawnee Tribe continues to work within these federal constraints. In the summer of 2002, they attempted to acquire the former Sunflower Army Ammunition plant in DeSoto, Kansas, southwest of Kansas City. The site is in former Shawnee territory, over which the tribe still has jurisdiction. The Sunflower plant manufactured ammunition from 1941 to 1993 and is now surplus army property—over ninety-five hundred acres of it. The tribe filed an injunction blocking the General Services Administration, the federal agency with oversight of the plant, from giving the property to anyone but the Shawnee Tribe of Oklahoma. The tribe has also put in a claim to the Bureau of Indian Affairs. If granted, this land will be put in trust for the tribe.

In 2002, tribal officials spoke of restoring native prairie and wildlife to about six thousand acres of the Sunflower property, and of adding a network of nature trails, nature education programs,

The Eastern Shawnee have adapted to today's world and own a number of businesses, like the People's National Bank in Seneca, Missouri.

and a center focusing on Kansas Indian history and Shawnee culture. Remaining property could be put toward commercial ventures.

By 2002, the Easterns had moved into banking, hospitality, and other enterprises. The tribe owns a Best Western motel in Fort Scott, Kansas and a People's Bank in Seneca, Missouri. Also in 2002, the Easterns worked on another ambitious project, a motel complex and truck plaza expected to open in 2005.

Today's Shawnee works at a modern career or runs a business. But the tribe's centuries-old tradition of communal and social responsibility continues, although now within the parameters of the white world.

Funding for Housing and Other Services

Tribal monies, as well as some federal dollars, fund programs covering housing, services for the aged, child care, meals, medical care, and social services. The Absentee provide tutoring for children ages four to six, and financial assistance for members attending college, graduate school, and summer school. In 2002, the Absentee started a program to help young tribal members with school expenses other than books or supplies. Any Absentee student could apply for tribal monies to be put toward academic trips, college classes that a high school student may enroll in, remedial classes, and college entrance exams.

Expanding tribal generosity into the area of health care, the tribe added a program geared to decrease the risk of diabetes and heart disease among Absentees. The program teaches participants about diet and exercise, and offers aerobic classes, fitness memberships at local health clubs, an annual Diabetes Kids' Camp, tests, and blood pressure readings.

The Absentees have also initiated charitable outreach far beyond their own community by donating monies to the Oklahoma City National Memorial, the Make A Wish Foundation, Big Brothers and Big Sisters, and Oklahoma youth sports organizations.

Eastern Shawnee services range from job hunt support to meals for senior tribal members. The Eastern housing authority, located north of tribal headquarters, helps people acquire and purchase housing. In 2002, the tribe was in the process of developing a neighborhood of forty homes on tribal land. The Eastern Shawnee also offer a school clothing allotment—two hundred dollars per child per school year—and child care, counseling, scholarships, and parenting classes for those members who need to study for a high school equivalency diploma. Health-care programs for the Eastern Shawnee include eyeglasses, prescription drugs, dental care, hearing aids, leg braces, and crutches. The tribe will also assist with college tuition for a total contribution of seventy-two hundred dollars per person.

As of 2002, the Shawnee Tribe was getting new community programs underway. But the delay in receiving federal recognition of tribal status has prevented most funding from the Native American Housing and Self Determination Act from reaching individual members. The tribe had also completed its application to participate in the Low Income Home Energy Assistance Project (LIHEAP), which makes money available for low income households to put toward heating and cooling costs. In 2002, the tribe partnered with a pharmaceutical network operated by the Mashantucket Pequot nation in Connecticut. By participating in this network, tribal members can obtain discounts on pharmaceuticals.

However, as economically viable as the three divisions of Shawnee have become, all realize that the survival of Shawnee culture is key to the survival of the Shawnee nation.

Reclaiming a Culture

A piece of Absentee Shawnee history stands in the form of a building at the Norman, Oklahoma, tribal complex: an old tuberculosis sanatorium that once treated Shawnee patients. Tuberculosis had become so prevalent among tribal youths and elders that the Shawnee Indian Sanatorium was opened to patients on December 10, 1924. The center had become the world's largest sanatorium for tubercular patients before it closed in 1962, a time when tuberculosis cases were beginning to decline in the United States. It was reopened as an Indian health clinic until 1979. Today, numerous tribal operations are conducted on the complex grounds.

About ten years ago the Eastern Shawnee added a special gathering place

Housing authority homes of the Eastern Shawnee tribe. The tribe provides a wealth of social programs to improve life for the Shawnee nation.

A Shawnee Artist

The work of a nineteenth-century Shawnee artist, Earnest Spybuck, is preserved in the Museum of the American Indian in New York and chronicles scenes from the daily life of the tribe after it was uprooted and forced to move west.

Born in 1883 in Oklahoma as a member of the Absentee Shawnee, Spybuck was self-taught as an artist. He made his first drawings in the dirt, using a stick, and later graduated to paper and pencil. His subject matter went well beyond Indian scenes: He drew cowboys, livestock, and the Western plains. In addition to a series he did on the Shawnee, Spybuck also painted ceremonials of neighboring tribes such as the Delaware and Sauk. His work was promoted and encouraged by an anthropologist for the Museum of the American Indian, which later acquired a good many of Spybuck's works.

Critics have said that while Spybuck was obviously untrained as an artist, he did demonstrate natural talent and captured in watercolors, his preferred medium, many traditional Shawnee ceremonies and customs. Spybuck, who died in 1948, painted such subject matter as a traditional men-against-women ball game, the opening of the Kispoko sacred bundle prior to a ceremonial war dance, the war dance itself, and a host of other Shawnee dances and games, such as the Stomp Dance, the Turkey Dance, and the Moccasin Game.

Earnest Spybuck was a nineteenth-century Shawnee artist who depicted daily Indian life.

to their tribal property: a powwow ground. Open and grassy, the powwow ground hosts dances, tribal ceremonies, and, of course, powwows. Powwows are a deeply rooted, very festive Indian tradition. They are occasions to gather and reconnect with friends. Native Americans of the eighteenth and nineteenth centuries would travel to powwows on foot or horseback; today's Shawnee are more likely to arrive in motorized vehicles.

Powwow traditions may differ among tribes but more likely than not a Shawnee powwow includes one or more drum groups, dancing, and traditional ceremonial clothing. Powwows have been identified as one of the means by which Indian tribes redistributed their resources and strengthened ties. It was also a way of building solidarity among tribal members.

Powwows could be held for any number of occasions. For example, one tribal member might give another member an important gift. In return, the recipient calls a powwow in his or her honor. Powwows have always been remarkably festive occasions. Today's Shawnee might simply attend powwows for the pleasure of the experience. They look forward to visiting with people they do not see very often, and enjoying the costumes, entertainment, and the sense of connection with their ancient culture.

Since 1991, the Eastern Shawnee have held an annual powwow, which has also been attended by members of the Absentees and the Shawnee Tribe. By 2002, this powwow had grown large enough to oc-cupy a special place on the tribal website, complete with photographs. The Eastern powwow includes traditional dances, such as the Stomp and Gourd Dances, prizes and contests for participants, and arts and crafts.

Planning for the Future, Honoring the Past

Every bit as important as the powwow are the tribe's efforts to preserve the Shawnee language. Only two hundred to five hundred fluent Shawnee speakers remain among the three tribal divisions. Preserving the tribe's native tongue has become an important goal for some members.

The Absentees have an ongoing language program and, in 2002, a not-for-profit enterprise known as Red Star was founded to help teach and preserve the Shawnee language. A linguist from the University of Kansas helped Red Star personnel develop a pronunciation key, workbook, audiotapes, and videotapes. Red Star also included teaching help from those who can still speak Shawnee fluently. Financial support for the program came from the Shawnee and from a Cherokee nation grant.

According to Shawnee officials, language preservation goes hand in hand with efforts to keep tribal history intact. With that in mind, council members from the Shawnee Tribe acquired property which encompasses the Kansas home and resting place of the Prophet, Tenkswatawa. This Shawnee Tribe site adjoins property owned by the Eastern Shawnee. An article in the winter edition of the 2001 *Shawnee Journal*, official newsletter of the Shawnee Tribe, explained the reasons for wanting the Prophet's home, and the process tribal members must now follow. According to the article,

> Tenkswatawa is of immense historical importance to all Shawnee, both in his own right and as Tecumseh's brother. Grants are being sought to acquire this property, located in the Argentine district of western Kansas City, to place it in trust for the Tribe [so that it no longer belongs to individual tribal members], and more importantly, to guarantee that the site is safeguarded forever.[43]

Members of the Shawnee nation hold on to their heritage in a myriad of ways, including how they do business. The tribe still conducts business by way of tribal council, though the council's leader is as likely to be called a chairman as he is a chief, and individual councils are also known as committees. The old peace and war

A Native American dances during a Shawnee powwow. A powwow is a traditional gathering featuring drums, dancing, and traditional ceremonial clothing.

chief designations are gone since the nation no longer officially declares war. But communal thinking and cooperation remain. And as the Shawnee face the twenty-first century, they are doing their best to begin thinking as a nation again.

Three Tribes, One Nation

The Shawnee have spent much of their history apart: first separated by the Beaver Wars, then by frequent migrations and conflicts with hostile Indians. Nonetheless, the Shawnee preserved a tribal identity. After resettlement in the Ohio River valley region the tribe would stand together against white settlers until three of the five clans decided they no longer wished to fight American expansion and moved west to Missouri. By the time the Ohio Shawnee were removed to Kansas and then Oklahoma, divisions of the tribe had lived apart for years, and were used to operating independently. Thus, the relations among the divisions were tense.

Yet, the three tribes of Shawnee have maintained a sense of community, particularly because so much intermarriage has occurred between divisions, and families can trace their roots back and forth between the different groups. Therefore, an Eastern powwow is likely to be attended by Absentees who will be able to greet many friends and relatives during the course of the ceremony. Since these strong ties are likely to continue, they may well bestow a sense of unity among the divisions as the Shawnee face the future.

Notes

Chapter 1: Wanderers and Warriors

1. John Sugden, *Blue Jacket, Warrior of the Shawnees*. Lincoln: University of Nebraska Press, 2000, p. 10.

2. Sugden, *Blue Jacket*, p. 22.

3. Quoted in Bil Gilbert, *God Gave Us This Country: Tekamthi and the First American Civil War*. New York: Atheneum, 1989, p. 47.

4. Christopher Gist, *Christopher Gist's Journals, with Commentary by William M. Darlington*. Pittsburgh: J.R. Weldin, 1893, p. 44.

5. Quoted in James H. Howard, *Shawnee! The Ceremonialism of a Native American Tribe and Its Cultural Background*. Athens: Ohio University Press, 1981, p. 76.

6. Quoted in Howard, *Shawnee!*, p. 83.

7. Joseph Rhodes, *Diary of Joseph and Martha Rhodes' Mission to the Shawnee Indians, 1817*. Columbus: Ohio Historical Society, p. 4.

8. Quoted in Sugden, *Blue Jacket*, p. 18.

9. Quoted in Lyman Copeland Draper, *The Draper Manuscripts: The Kenton Papers*, Series BB, vol. 2. Madison: Wisconsin Historical Society, circa 1840.

10. Quoted in Draper, *The Draper Manuscripts: The Kenton Papers*, Series BB, vol. 2.

Chapter 2: Becoming Shawnee

11. Quoted in Howard, *Shawnee!*, p. 71.

12. Quoted in Howard, *Shawnee!*, p. 48.

13. Quoted in William A. Galloway, *Old Chillicothe, Shawnee, and Pioneer History: Conflicts and Romances in the Northwest Territory*. Xenia, OH: The Buckeye Press, 1934, p. 184.

14. Quoted in Howard, *Shawnee!*, p. 56.

15. Gilbert, *God Gave Us This Country*, p. 8.

16. Gilbert, *God Gave Us This Country*, p. 9.

17. Quoted in Galloway, *Old Chillicothe, Shawnee, and Pioneer History*, p. 195.

18. Quoted in Galloway, *Old Chillicothe, Shawnee, and Pioneer History*, p. 173.

19. Quoted in Gilbert, *God Gave Us This Country*, p. 20.

20. Quoted in Gilbert, *God Gave Us This Country*, p. 21.

21. Quoted in Howard, *Shawnee!*, p. 109.

Chapter 3: Spirits and Shamans

22. Quoted in Howard, *Shawnee!*, p. 144.

23. Quoted in Galloway, *Old Chillicothe, Shawnee, and Pioneer History*, p. 176.

24. Gilbert, *God Gave Us This Country*, p. 217.

25. David Jones, *A Journal of Two Visits Made to Some Nations of Indians on the West Side of the River Ohio in the*

Years 1772 and 1773. Chillicothe, OH: Ross County Historical Society, 1946, p. 11.

26. Rhodes, *Diary of Joseph and Martha Rhodes' Mission*, p. 2.

Chapter 4: Homecoming and Loss

27. Quoted in Draper, *The Draper Manuscripts: Draper's Life of Boone*, Series B, vol. 1.

28. Quoted in John Bennett, *Blue Jacket, War Chief of the Shawnees and His Part in Ohio's History*. Chillicothe, OH: Ross County Historical Society, 1943, p. 10.

29. Sudgen, *Blue Jacket,* p. 13.

30. Reuben Gold Thwaite, *Afloat on the Ohio.* Carbondale: Southern Illinois University Press, 1897, p. 153.

31. Quoted in Draper, *The Draper Manuscripts: Border Wars*, Series D, vol. 2, p. 111.

32. Thwaite, *Afloat on the Ohio*, p. 129.

33. Quoted in Gilbert, *God Gave Us This Country*, p. 69.

Chapter 5: Tecumseh, the Prophet, and Exile in the West

34. Rhodes, *Diary of Joseph and Martha Rhodes' Mission*, p. 3.

35. Quoted in Gilbert, *God Gave Us This Country*, p. 214.

36. Gilbert, *God Gave Us This Country*, p. 314.

37. John Sugden, *Tecumseh: A Life.* New York: Henry Holt, 1997, p. 387.

38. Rhodes, *Diary of Joseph and Martha Rhodes' Mission*, p. 5.

39. Quoted in Gilbert, *God Gave Us This Country*, p. 332.

40. Flora Kittle, *The Shawnee Indians in Kansas.* Indianapolis: 1917, p. 10.

41. Quoted in Gilbert, *God Gave Us This Country*, p. 51.

Chapter 6: A Nation Continues

42. Quoted in Lora Abaurrea, "Gambling on Indian Reservations," May 6, 1996. www.sims.berkeley.edu, p. 4.

43. *Shawnee Journal*, vol. 1, no. 1, Winter 2001, p. 5.

For Further Reading

Books

Lydia Bjornlund, *The Iroquois*. San Diego: Lucent Books, 2001. Part of Lucent Books's Indigenous Peoples of North America series, *The Iroquois* tells of the five-nation confederacy that, while a powerful foe of the Shawnee, practiced a mostly agricultural lifestyle that centered around the longhouse, where most decisions were made.

Robert Cwiklik, *Tecumseh: Shawnee Rebel*. New York: Chelsea House, 1993. Part of the publisher's North American Indians of Achievement series, this biography of Tecumseh is presented partially in a narrative format with emphasis, not surprisingly, on Tecumseh's conflicts with the whites. Tecumseh's brother, the Prophet, is also discussed.

Allen W. Eckert, *The Frontiersmen*. Boston: Little Brown, 1967. Although Eckert takes some liberties with his narrative by re-creating conversations for which there were no witnesses, he provides a solid account of the Ohio frontier, including the Draper Manuscripts.

Mary R. Furbee, *Shawnee Captive: The Story of Mary Draper Ingles*. Greensboro, NC: Morgan Reynolds, 2001. Mary Draper Ingles and her children were kidnapped from their West Virginia home by a party of Shawnee warriors in 1775. She and a fellow prisoner eventually escaped, traveling the eight-hundred-mile trek to West Virginia on foot, using the Ohio River and its tributaries as their guide. Furbee's biography of Ingles tells of her life before and after her capture, and provides a detailed account of one of the more harrowing journeys in pioneer history.

Barbara Graymont, *The Iroquois in the American Revolution*. Syracuse, NY: Syracuse University Press, 1972. Advanced readers who want a closer look at the American Indian role in the American Revolution might wish to read this well-researched book.

Though mostly about the Iroquois, who were British allies, the book also discusses the Shawnee role in the conflict, as well as that of other Indian tribes.

Judith Harlen, *American Indians Today: Issues and Conflicts.* New York: Franklin Watts, 1987. Though not a specific look at the Shawnee, this book does give an overview of the many challenges American Indians face in modern society. Also describes the removal of eastern Indian tribes onto reservations. The book includes photographs of Indians in a modern environment.

Janet Hubbard-Brown, *The Shawnee.* New York: Chelsea House, 1995. Hubbard-Brown's young adult book on the Shawnee is a good primer for those who want an overview of the Shawnee nation and its history. This book includes current and historic photographs, paintings, and a glossary.

Myra H. Immell and William H. Immell, *The Importance of Tecumseh.* San Diego: Lucent Books, 1997. This young adult book, part of Lucent Books's Importance Of biography series, focuses on Tecumseh as a leader and a man, discussing his life, policies, ideas, hopes for his nation, and place in history.

Louis P. Masur, *1831: Year of Eclipse.* New York: Hill and Wang, 2001. Mature readers who want a more in-depth and unconventional look at the era of the Indian Removal Act will enjoy Masur's book. It offers a literary snapshot of a very difficult year in American history, one that also included Nat Turner's Rebellion. The book provides lesser known details on the Indian Removal Act, including that many white Americans opposed it.

Pat McCarthy, *Daniel Boone: Frontier Legend.* Berkeley Heights, NJ: Enslow, 2000. McCarthy's young adult book, good for readers new to frontier history, describes the life and times of Daniel Boone, America's most famous frontiersman and a pioneer who spent a good deal of time dealing with the Shawnee Indians. McCarthy's book worships Boone a bit, but contains good, basic information sure to intrigue middle school students.

Carl Waldman, *Atlas of the North American Indian.* New York: Facts On File, 1985. Although dry at times, this well-illustrated book on Indian tribes in North America includes plenty of infor-

mation on the Shawnee in their Ohio homeland, as well as the
Shawnee lands in Kansas and Oklahoma. Maps and illustrations
are by Molly Braun. The book also includes a discussion of U.S.
Indian policy through the 1980s and early 1990s.

Websites

Ohio Indians Learning Links (www.oplin.lib.oh.us). The
Shawnee had a host of Ohio allies, including the Miami, Wyan-
dot, and Delaware. This website details the history of those tribes
as well as the Shawnee, and highlights some major Ohio Indian
battles.

The Shawnee—A Profile (www.merceronline.com). This site features a brief tribal history, with links to sites on the Cherokee and
on Indian folk tales and legends.

Shawnee Indians (www.ohiokids.org). This website is a good
primer on tribal history, written for middle school and younger
students, and includes links to other sites important to Shawnee
history.

Works Consulted

Books

John Bennett, *Blue Jacket, War Chief of the Shawnees and His Part in Ohio's History*. Chillicothe, OH: Ross County Historical Society, 1943. Bennett's brief biography supports the traditional view that Blue Jacket was, in fact, white. His work includes a brief anecdote whereby the Shawnee chief allegedly encountered one of his white cousins, Eleanor Swearingen, who had married Ohio senator Thomas Worthington.

William A. Galloway, *Old Chillicothe, Shawnee, and Pioneer History: Conflicts and Romances in the Northwest Territory*. Xenia, OH: The Buckeye Press, 1934. Galloway is a descendant of one of Ohio's most prominent pioneer families. This Ohio history book includes a lengthy essay by Shawnee writer Thomas Wildcat Alford, in which he describes the customs, religious practices, and daily activities of the Shawnee.

Bil Gilbert, *God Gave Us This Country: Tekamthi and the First American Civil War*. New York: Atheneum, 1989. Gilbert's biography of Shawnee chief Tecumseh focuses not only on the great chief's life, but on environmental, economic, and social issues associated with the Shawnee tribe. Gilbert prefers to use an alternate spelling of the chief's name, Tekamthi, throughout the book.

Christopher Gist, *Christopher Gist's Journals, with Commentary by William M. Darlington*. Pittsburgh: J.R. Weldin, 1893. Gist, an agent of the Ohio Company of Virginia, explored the greater part of the Ohio, Kentucky, western Maryland, and southwestern Pennsylvania region in 1750 and 1751. His journals are the first accounts of daily life in Shawnee country.

James H. Howard, *Shawnee! The Ceremonialism of a Native American Tribe and Its Cultural Background*. Athens: Ohio University Press, 1981. Although several of Howard's conclusions regarding tribal culture and religion are disputed by some modern Shawnee, he makes good use of very early manuscripts describing white encounters with the tribe.

David Jones, *A Journal of Two Visits Made to Some Nations of Indians on the West Side of the River Ohio in the Years 1772 and 1773*. Chillicothe, OH: Ross County Historical Society, 1946. Jones, a New Jersey minister, visited the Ohio territory in 1773 and 1774 determined to convert the Shawnee to Christianity. His efforts were rebuffed, but he stayed long enough to write a detailed, albeit colorful, account of their daily lives.

Flora Kittle, *The Shawnee Indians in Kansas*. Indianapolis: 1917. Kittle provides a brief history of Quaker missionary involvement with the Shawnee tribe in Johnson County, Kansas. It also includes diary excerpts from Matilda Smith, a young teacher in the 1850s. The manuscript was published in pamphlet form as a means to raise money for an ill Kansas boy who was the grandson of mission teachers.

John Sugden, *Blue Jacket, Warrior of the Shawnees*. Lincoln: University of Nebraska Press, 2000. Sugden's biography takes the more current view that Blue Jacket was not a white man but a Shawnee born and raised. In addition to detailing what is known of the chief's life, Sugden's book also includes extensive discussions of Shawnee culture, history, and religious ceremonies.

———, *Tecumseh: A Life*. New York: Henry Holt, 1997. Blue Jacket biographer Sugden adds his take on the life of Tecumseh, a famous Shawnee chief. Sugden also describes the latter days of Tecumseh's brother, Tenkswatawa, who fell from power and influence after Tecumseh's death.

Reuben Gold Thwaite, *Afloat on the Ohio*. Carbondale: Southern Illinois University Press, 1897. Thwaite, a *Wisconsin State Journal* editor, traveled one thousand miles along the Ohio River during the waning days of the nineteenth century. In addition to the travel commentary, Thwaite provides information on important historical events that took place during his travels.

Erminie Wheeler Voegelin, *Mortuary Customs of the Shawnee and Other Eastern Tribes*. Indianapolis: Indiana Historical Society, 1944. Voegelin provides a tremendous amount of detail on Shawnee burial practices, comparing them to the burial customs of the other Woodland tribes.

Periodicals

Shawnee Journal, vol. 1, no. 1, Winter 2001, and vol. 1, no. 2, summer 2002. The official newsletter of the Shawnee Tribe of Oklahoma, who were formerly known as the Loyal or Cherokee Shawnee. The newsletters announce events and happenings, as well as chronicle the tribe's attempts at economic development.

Unpublished Materials

Lyman Copeland Draper, *The Draper Manuscripts*. Madison: Wisconsin Historical Society, circa 1840. In the 1830s and 1840s, Lyman Draper gathered as much factual information as possible on the history of the Ohio frontier from those who had either witnessed it or knew the participants well. Draper's interviewees were primarily white. His collection includes not only his handwritten notes but personal documents from the likes of Daniel Boone, George Rogers Clark, Simon Kenton, and others. The Draper Manuscripts are kept in a series of bound volumes, including *Draper's Life of Boone, Border Wars,* and *The Kenton Papers.*

Joseph Rhodes, *Diary of Joseph and Martha Rhodes' Mission to the Shawnee Indians, 1817.* Columbus: Ohio Historical Society. Joseph Rhodes kept a diary of his brief sojourn among the Shawnee during the post-Tecumseh era. His wife Martha and daughter Amy accompanied him on what was supposed to be a Christian mission to the Indians. Tragically, Martha died just months after their arrival, prompting Joseph and Amy to head eastward for home. Father and daughter stayed long enough for Joseph to record his observations of Shawnee society, for which he had much sympathy. The journal was transcribed and typewritten from its handwritten original by one of the Rhodes's great-granddaughters. It is part of the Ohio Historical Society's permanent collection.

Internet Sources

Lora Abaurrea, "Gambling on Indian Reservations," May 6, 1996. www.sims.berkeley.edu.

Mary Wahpepah, "Absentee Shawnee Tribe Helps Fund Local Charities," *Shawnee News-Star*, May 2000. www.news-star.com.

Websites

The Absentee Shawnee Tribe of Oklahoma (www.absentee shawneetribe.com). The official website of the Absentee Shawnee Tribe of Oklahoma lists local tribal officials, tribal projects, and a description of the tribe's major economic endeavor, the Thunderbird Casino.

Eastern Shawnee Tribe of Oklahoma (http://showcase. netins.net). This very detailed website of the Eastern Shawnee details their economic development projects and their cultural and social service activities.

History of the Shawnee Indian Mission Historic Site, Kansas State Historical Society (www.kshs.org). The Shawnee mission, run by Methodist missionaries, gave a Western education to young Shawnee and children from other Indian tribes in the period before the Civil War. The site is now maintained by the Kansas State Historical Society.

Shawnee History (www.tolatsga.org). This very long and dense account of the Shawnee traces their earliest beginnings in Ohio and follows tribal history from the Beaver Wars to the tribe's removal to the West.

The Shawnee Tribe (www.shawnee-tribe.org). This is the official website of the Shawnee Tribe, once known as the Loyal or Cherokee Shawnee. The website details tribal news and programs as well as Shawnee history.

United Remnant Band of Shawnees, Ohio (www.shawneeurb. homestead.com). This group of Ohio Shawnee is recognized by neither the federal government nor the three Shawnee divisions of Oklahoma. Yet, it has attained recognition from the state of Ohio and maintains several tribal enterprises, including a website.

Index

Picture Credits

About the Author

Mary C. Wilds, author of *Indigenous Peoples of Southeast Asia* for Lucent Books, is an author and playwright who has also penned a series of young adult biographies, including *Forgotten Champion: The Story of Major Taylor, Fastest Bicycle Rider in the World*. She lives in Indiana.